Small Town
Big Miracle

BISHOP **W.C. MARTIN**
WITH JOHN FORNOF

Tyndale House Publishers, Inc.
Carol Stream, Illinois

Editor: Marianne Hering
Cover design by Joseph Sapulich
Cover photograph of people by Tyndale House Publishers. All rights reserved.
Cover treatments by iStockphoto. All rights reserved.
Interior photos by John Fornof unless otherwise noted.

Library of Congress Cataloging-in-Publication Data
Martin, W. C., 1946-
    Small town, big miracle / by W. C. Martin with John Fornof.
        p. cm.
    "A Focus on the Family book."
    ISBN-13: 978-1-58997-443-2
    ISBN-10: 1-58997-443-3
    1. Church work with children—Texas—Possum Trot. 2. Bennett Chapel (Possum
Trot, Tex.) 3. Foster home care—Texas—Possum Trot. 4. Adoption—Religious
aspects—Christianity. 5. Abused children—Texas. I. Fornof, John, 1960- II. Title.
    BV639.C4M37 2007
    261.8'327109764179—dc22
                                                        2007012928
Printed in the United States of America
    3 4 5 6 7 8 9 / 13 12 11 10 09

I would like to thank God for the opportunity to present to the world this treasure. I echo the words of King David: "The LORD has done this, and it is marvelous in our eyes" (Psalm 118:23). I thank God for my parents, L. M. and Pearline Martin, for teaching me the value of family. I also thank God for my lovely wife, Donna; my children—Terry, Princeton, La'Donna, Joshua, Tyler, Mercedes, and Terri; grandson, No'ah A'Mhad; my sister and nine brothers; Bennett Chapel Church family; and Saving a Generation Ministry.

May God bless and keep you; you are in our prayers.

—Bishop W. C. Martin

I give glory and honor to God for all my many blessings. God has truly been awesome in my life. This book is dedicated in the loving memory of my wonderful parents, L. J. Cartwright and Murtha Lee Grisby Cartwright. Special thanks to my godparents, Bishop and Mother Liz Swindle. Neither this book nor my ministry would have been possible without their love and dedication to our family. It's because of their deep love for family values and the Word of God that I am the person who I am today. Many blessings and thanks to the entire Cartwright and Grisby families. Your love and support means the world to me. "[I am] confident of this, that he who began a good work in you will carry it on to completion until the day of Christ Jesus" (Philippians 1:6).

—Donna Martin

"And the King will answer and say to them,

'Assuredly, I say to you, inasmuch

as you did it to one of the least of these

My brethren, you did it to Me.' "

—MATTHEW 25:40 (NKJV)

Contents

Acknowledgments

In addition to acknowledging the Holy Spirit for guiding and directing our steps, we wish to note the help we've received from these individuals, corporations, and media entities.

Individuals:

Bishop Shelton Beatty, Valerie Huscher Bell, Judy Bowman-Pitts, Kim Burell, Speaker of the House Tom Delay, Pastor Walter G. Diggler, Pastor W. L. Dunn, Hilary Field, Dr. Glory J. Floyd, Bishop T. D. Jakes, Joyce James, Dremus David Lifshutz, Ruth G. McRoy, Bishop Paul S. Morton, Bishop G. E. Patterson, Dr. Reverend John R. Steward, Donald Trump, Be Be Winans, Dr. Robert L. Woodson, Pastor Remus Wright.

Corporations:

Armstrong Wood Products; Bennett Chapel Church Family; Bethany Christian Services; Center Independent School District in Center, Texas, it's officials and citizens; Covington Lumber Company; Mount of Olives Lutheran Church of Mission Viejo, California; New Pleasant Grove Baptist Church of Houston; Oil of Joy Ministries I and II; Spalding Christian Services.

Media Entities

48 Hours; ABC's *Good Morning America; Caring People* magazine; *Christian Readers* magazine; Essence Award Ceremony, Fox Television Network; *Essence* magazine; *Family Circle* magazine; BBC Radio; KIRB TV, Houston; Korean Television, 20-minute report; NBC, *The Spirit of Giving;* NBC's Extra; *The Oprah Winfrey Show; Orange County (California) Register; People* magazine; *Readers Digest; Renovate My Family; Texas Monthly* magazine; Trinity Broadcast Network; *Woman's World* magazine.

—Bishop W. C. and Donna Martin

Thank you to Bishop Zephaniah Swindle, who provided the wonderful historic tours and tales of Possum Trot, Texas, and to Kerry Cartwright for his friendship and insight into the heart of this community.

Thank you to the amazing people of Possum Trot for their patience through many hours of interviews, and for opening their hearts and homes.

Thank you, Larry Weeden, for your trust and inspiration for this project, and thanks also to Marianne Hering for your encouragement and passion for excellence.

And most of all, thank You, God, for entrusting us to tell such a special story.

—John Fornof

Introduction

The dark spots on her legs told a story of abuse. The pattern of discoloration on her skin confirmed she had been burned with a cigarette lighter. Reports say she passed out from the pain. She was dumped in a ditch, left to die.

She was three years old. Her name is Terri.

She's my daughter.

To some people, Terri and others like her are considered broken. They were abandoned, abused, and traumatized at an early age. When they're older, they suffer from all kinds of behavior problems. Most people see them as throwaways. Nobody wants to adopt problem kids like these.

Nobody, that is, except people like us.

This is our story—the story of how God inspired Possum Trot, Texas, to take on 72 of the toughest kids from the foster-care system and adopt them as their own. It's also the story of how God has used our little community of three hundred folks to spark the conscience of a nation.

Our kids didn't come to us as cute little Gerber babies. They came to us rough, right off the street, and right into our homes, where they lied to us, cheated us, and stole from us. They were— and still can be—masters of manipulation. It's how they learned to survive. Our kids were abandoned by their mamas, left at home with nothing to eat. They had to sneak food from the store just to put something in their tummies. Some of our kids were beaten by drunk daddies. Some were raped. These are little children I'm talking about.

And that's where the heroes come in. You're going to meet some of them. These aren't television celebrities. These are real-life heroes. Take the Browns, for instance. Here's a grandmother and grandfather—with kids already grown—who decided to adopt *triplets! Two-year-old* triplets! You'll also meet Diann Sparks—a single working mom—who adopted two boys as her own. And the Lathans—Lord have mercy! Wait till you hear what happened to *them.* But I'm getting ahead of myself.

You might have heard parts of our story already. God blessed us with opportunities to appear on NBC *News,* ABC's *Good Morning America,* and CBS. My wife and I even got to be on *The Oprah Winfrey Show.* You might've seen us written up in *Reader's Digest* or *People* or *Family Circle* or *Southern Living.*

It's quite a blessing. It's quite a story. It's the miracle of Possum Trot, Texas.

One

At the End of the Pavement

Welcome to Possum Trot, Texas! I'm guessing you're from a long ways away, because any place is a long ways from Possum Trot.

Take a look around you. You'll see well-kept, double-wide mobile homes with neatly mowed acres of grass, where kids laugh and run. And you'll see clapboard shacks sprawled out on bald knobs of dirt, where rusted-out pickup trucks serve as lawn ornaments.

Just up the road is Bennett Chapel, my church; I'm the pastor, W. C. Martin.

You may think of us as poor, maybe less educated than you. Deep in the shadow of your soul, you may even look down on us. But whatever you do, don't dismiss us or you'll miss the treasure.

3

It's the secret of how we overcame huge challenges to raise 72 adopted kids. Many adoptions end up in what social services calls "disillusionment." But here in Possum Trot, after more than 10 years and all these kids, not one child has been sent back to the system.

I challenge you to look beyond your first impressions, dig a little deeper, and discover the hidden wealth here, because this is someplace special, even though you might not recognize it . . . yet.

Our community is an important character in this story. It's part of our miracle. So, hop in the truck and strap on your seatbelt. As we say here in the South, you're "fixin' to" get a personal tour of Possum Trot, Texas.

First off, you'll notice there aren't any signs that say "Possum Trot." And you won't find it on most maps, either. It's like a lost treasure. We're in East Central Texas, about 10 miles from the border of Louisiana, right on the edge of the Sabine National Forest.

Some people in surrounding areas refer to Possum Trot as the place "back in the woods." Social workers had their doubts if the rough and tough kids from the foster system could make it in this tiny community. Could the people here really pull this off?

They weren't the only ones who doubted. I wish I could tell you that when my wife, Donna, first mentioned adoption, an unexplainable thrill went through my being . . . that I put my arms around her and told her we were in this new adventure together and I would support her in any way I could.

Actually, my exact words were, "Yeah, right!"

But I have to be honest. Adoption just didn't make sense for us. I called myself a man of faith, but right then I had a lot of doubts. We already had two kids, 9-year-old LaDonna and our 15-year-old son, Princeton, who has been permanently brain-damaged since birth. It didn't fit our family to adopt.

We were pastoring a church while I was working a full-time job in insurance and supervising the construction of a new church building. We were way too busy.

Donna was emotionally burdened—still recovering from a personal tragedy. The timing wasn't right to adopt.

But God told us to adopt anyway. This decision wasn't about our lifestyle or our schedule or our timing. Really, it wasn't about us at all. This decision was about the children.

We didn't realize it at the time, but Princeton was actually God's preparation for us. He was born with brain damage after my wife went through 18 hours of intense labor. The doctors said Prince would never amount to anything more than a "vegetable," and they advised us to make him a ward of the state. But Princeton was our *son*. We took him home with us.

Through Princeton, God taught us what patience and long-suffering were all about. We were sure God was going to heal him. We prayed so hard. He had seizures. He'd fall and bust his head. It was a hard sight—our son all bruised up like that.

But we wouldn't give up.

See, God taught us not to give up on anything. So we refused to quit. It was a full-time job just keeping up with the boy, but we stayed with him. We kept on praying.

When Princeton was about 7 years old, God healed him of the seizures! He still has brain damage, but he's also one of the musicians at the church, where he plays bass guitar. And now Princeton is the one who prays for others—all because we wouldn't give up.

See, God was training us for a ministry we couldn't envision quite yet. He was preparing us to take in kids who needed so much. Kids who were damaged through no fault of their own. Kids who needed lots of patience. Kids who needed lots of love.

Of course, when you go through tough times, you don't always see the full picture. At the time, adoption just didn't make sense at all. But God took us back to where I'm taking you now. It's a place of inspiration that God used to change our minds. And change our lives.

We'll take a right turn here on County Road 2625. You notice there aren't any paved roads in Possum Trot. Just red dirt and black gravel winding through green, piney woods. Deep in these very woods—off to the right a ways—is the little white four-room house where the miracle of Possum Trot really started.

Donna is already there to meet us. I want you to hear the story from her, because she tells it best. Folks around here call her "Sister Martin" or "First Lady."

I met Donna when I was touring with my brothers—the Martin Brothers—singing all across the country. We stopped here

Donna Martin on her back porch

in Possum Trot for a concert at a little wooden church called Bennett Chapel. Little did I know I would pastor this same church some day. But something I did know right away: The young lady who walked in the door while I was singing was going to be my wife. I fell in love with her.

I believe you will too.

Here's Donna's story:

I can still see my mama sitting in her rocking chair there on our front porch. I can still hear her humming. I can still feel her arms around me as I sat quietly in her lap as a little girl, my head against her breast, listening.

In moments like those, lessons were inscribed on my heart—lessons that inspired me to one day adopt little ones who were strangers to love.

A small shack with a dirt-floor porch was home to 18 kids in all. No electricity. No running water. We had to wash our clothes in a Number 3 tin tub. We had an outhouse and a little pot inside we called the pee pot. We'd put pine oil in it and keep a lid on it.

Somehow, some way, Mama made that shack a home. Even with 18 kids, Mama never screamed at us, never cussed, never talked down to us. But you never crossed her either.

Of course, we didn't have any health insurance or money for a doctor. So when we were little and we'd get sick, we'd just look to Mama. Toothache, headache, mumps, whatever. I can remember one time when I was five or six years old, I got real sick. My head was hurting me so badly, I started to cry.

Mama picked me up and sat me in her lap. And she began to rock me in that rocking chair of hers and just started humming. Then she prayed. I closed my eyes. The tears streamed down my face. And in the quietness of that moment, there in Mama's arms, I was healed! The headache went away!

Mama's love brought us through the tough stuff. I learned that if anything will take you through, love will.

Mama took in strangers and fed them as well, because folks knew there was always food at her house. She treated the "take ins" as family. If they were about to get in trouble, they knew they could go talk to Mama. She wasn't just Mama at home. She was "Mama" to all of Possum Trot.

On February 12, 1996, right about two o'clock in the afternoon, I got a call from my brother Kerry. Mama was in the hospital. In the emergency room. A few minutes later, one of the people from the church called. "First Lady, you really need to go now. She's in cardiac arrest."

When I got to the hospital, my niece Rachel met me in the parking lot. But she never said a word. Once inside, I saw the emergency doors were shut. The curtains were closed. My auntie, Cora Williams, came out and hugged me. "Well," she said, "we just lost Murtha."

And I looked at her.

"Lost Mama?"

"Yes. Mother just passed away."

I turned. All I could do was run.

And scream.

This wasn't right. I was the First Lady of the church. It was my job to pray for people, encourage them, go to prayer meetings, help lead the worship service, visit the sick, be strong for others, give people hope. It was my job to hold things together. Now I was falling apart.

I pushed my feelings down deep and pushed on with life. But the feelings of pain were still there. For several months after Mama died, I was out in my yard every day planting flowers, lots of them. I set the most beautiful flower garden, alive with color, fresh with fragrance. It was my way of crowding out the ugly weeds of pain and emptiness that kept choking me.

One morning I was alone in the house. I stood in the kitchen washing dishes when that all-too-familiar dark shadow crossed over me again—a shadow of pain, anger, emptiness. I had had enough. "Okay, God," I said. "Today is the day. I have complained to you, I've cried, I've ached, I've hurt . . ." I looked up through my kitchen ceiling, right into heaven, right into His heart. And I said, "God, You either heal me, or let me die."

As soon as I spoke those words, I was moved to step out on my back porch. As I stood looking out over my back yard filled with flowers, I felt the Holy Spirit say something to me.

"I hear you."

His words fed my spirit. "I've heard your pain, and I've heard your complaints. But I want you to take a moment and think about all those children out there who do not have what you had in a mother. I want you to give back to them. Foster and adopt."

Immediately, a sense of healing came over me. I was overtaken by the light, the warmth, and the presence of my God. The dark shadow fled as quickly as a fog when the morning sun splits through.

I didn't know a thing about adoption. But I went into the house and called the number I found in the phone book. I stood in the kitchen on the phone and spoke 11 words that changed my life.

"I'm Donna Martin, and I want to become a foster parent."

Two

The First of 72

I thought Donna had flipped out.

You see, Donna is project oriented. She'll start enthusiastically on a wonderful project or a great cause, then she'll start another one, and another, till she gets burned out. To me, researching adoption was just another "Donna project." She was still struggling with extended grief over her mother's death. Although adoption was a noble idea, I didn't think this notion would last long.

But something was different this time. Something was different about Donna. I saw a fire in her I had never seen before. This time, she wasn't going to let go. She wasn't going to give up.

I respect the quality of perseverance in anyone—especially my wife. That's because perseverance is in my roots as well. I had trouble in school and flunked several times. Many people said I would never finish high school. But I was determined. I was 21 years old when I graduated. I later went on to seminary in

13

Houston and received a bachelor's degree, then a master's in theology. I would wake up at five in the morning, work 10 to 12 hours a day as a lead man and supervisor at Reed Tool Company, then head off for seminary till 10 that night. Then on weekends, I'd drive three and a half hours from Houston to Possum Trot to preach at Bennett Chapel.

When I saw this same kind of perseverance in Donna, it started me thinking: *Maybe this isn't just a Donna project. Maybe this is a God project. And maybe adoption—somehow—can finally bring the healing she so desperately needs.*

Finally, I said okay.

Donna asked her sister Diann to take the adoption classes with her for moral support. Diann's first response was, "Girl, you're crazy." But in the end, she came around. "If God said for you to do it, we'll do it together."

It was a three-hour class every week and meant driving more than 120 miles round trip to Lufkin, Texas. It lasted 13 weeks. Diann was there simply to support Donna because for Diann, adoption wasn't an option. "I was a single working mom," she said. "I already had a daughter at home. I didn't think I could do it."

But something happened as Diann and Donna listened to caseworkers tell stories about kids who were abused emotionally, physically, or sexually. And the caseworkers didn't sugarcoat what could happen once adoptive parents brought these kids into their homes. "They may start a fire in your house. They may steal from you, lie to you, tear your house up. They don't understand love, so they're going to create all kinds of chaos."

Donna looked at her sister. Their eyes met. They had no words, but their eyes said to each other, "We can do this." They thought back to what their mama taught them through her example. "Love can do it."

I waved good-bye to Donna as she drove to these classes every week, and I listened to her describe the rough realities of adoption. Donna still maintained hope. And I started making the drive with Donna and her sister. Something was happening inside me as well.

Although Donna got the word from the Holy Spirit first, Diann became the first parent to adopt in our community. Four-year-old Nino arrived in Possum Trot in October 1997. The miracle had begun.

MERCEDES AND TYLER

February 1997 marked one year since Donna's mama had died. That month Donna got word from some foster parents about two beautiful biracial kids—a five-year-old girl named Mercedes and her little two-year-old brother, Tyler. The foster parents told Donna up front that Mercedes was having lots of problems at kindergarten.

Donna had been wanting a girl and a boy. Were these the ones? Here's what she remembers about her first encounter:

The foster mother told me I could go to the school and see Mercedes. I walked onto the playground, and kids came running up to me—kids from our church. "Sister Martin, what are you doing here?" they asked.

"I'm looking for a little girl named Mercedes. Do you know her?" They pointed to a thin, five-year-old girl. She was standing by herself on a pile of rocks. Her little face was gorgeous, her skin a warm coffee with lots of cream.

She was barefoot. She had taken off her tennis shoes and was filling them with rocks and pouring them out. I walked up to her.

"Hey, little girl. What's your name?" I expected her to be shy, but I was met with an unexpected warmth.

"Hi. My name is Mercedes."

"Such a beautiful name for such a beautiful girl." I smiled at her and then asked, "Why are you playing all by yourself?"

"I don't know. Nobody wants to play with me."

"I can't believe no one would want to play with you." I looked her in the eyes. "I want you to know you are beautiful. I'm gonna go now. And I look forward to seeing you again, okay?"

"Okay . . ."

I went to the teacher, sitting by her classroom. As soon as I mentioned Mercedes, the teacher shook her head. "Oh, she has so many problems."

"What kind of problems?"

"She steals the children's candy, lunch, whatever, and so no one wants to play with her."

Somewhere inside of me, a determined thought came to mind: We're going to change all that. *I drove back home, and I prayed the whole way.*

When I had looked into that baby's eyes, I just knew. I knew she was my child. It was also clear that something wasn't right. I was convinced that her problem was with the adults around her, not the children. Looking back now, I had no idea.

My husband called Susan Ramsey, our caseworker. "What about Mercedes and Tyler?" Susan was a remarkably kind woman, but she was upset. She pointed out that the foster mother had had no right to call or discuss anything about this child. And there was a bigger problem at stake.

"Reverend Martin and Donna, I respect you so much. But I cannot put this child in your home." She was concerned that after my mother's death I might not be able to take on these kids. "It's going to be a disruption."

I respected Susan, but I knew these were my children. However, she refused to budge. Pastor called Susan's boss, Judy Bowman. And she agreed with Susan's assessment. The government was saying no.

Still, we didn't give up. We asked folks everywhere to pray. Meantime, Susan was sidelined with serious health issues and Judy took over the case.

One day I was in the shower, getting ready to go to a conference, when I heard the phone ring. Pastor answered it. He burst in the bathroom. "Donna, God has moved. That's Judy Bowman on the phone. We're gonna get the children tomorrow!" Apparently, God spoke to Judy and changed her mind. But this was only our first challenge to overcome.

Mercedes didn't want to go into a black family. She didn't want a black mom or dad. She was told that all blacks were real poor, they didn't have food to eat, and they didn't have TV. What they did have were rats and roaches.

When I got back from grocery shopping, Tyler and Mercedes were there in our driveway. I got out of my car and called out, "Mercedes!" I ran to her and held her real, real tight. And there was two-year-old Tyler, with soft curly hair. Still in diapers. And very, very quiet.

I gave them a tour through our home and showed them their rooms. "See? You have your own room, and look, we have a TV." I took Mercedes to the kitchen and showed her the cabinets packed full of food.

And I reassured her. "I'll be the best mom to you that I could ever be. I will be there for you, for whatever. You can never do anything to take away my love for you. We're here for the long haul."

REALITY SETS IN

I had already said yes. But reality was starting to hit. Now that the kids were here, the old fears came back as well. What was this going to do to Donna? She was overloaded as it was with Princeton, plus the church responsibilities, plus the family responsibilities, plus the grief over her mother, plus . . .

As for me, I was a full-time dad, a full-time pastor, and a full-time insurance salesman. My life was already full time . . . big time. Could I really give Tyler and Mercedes the time they needed? On top of that, we had been warned about the emotional baggage these kids had and how they could totally disrupt a family. How would taking in these kids affect Princeton and LaDonna?

The questions swirled around like a whirlwind inside me. How could I do this? Could I really, truly help them? Did I really have the time, the energy, and the stuff it took to be the father these kids needed?

I was facing adult-sized qualms and fears. But that day when Tyler and Mercedes first arrived, Tyler came to me at a full run. "Hey, Daddy!" This handsome, curly-headed little guy jumped up into my arms.

And it was all over. All my fears melted away with the hug of a little boy. I held him in my arms, and my life changed. Somehow, I knew we were going to make it.

After Donna gave Mercedes and Tyler the tour of our home, we all sat down to eat. And I was dumbfounded. These two kids stuffed food into their little mouths as if it were going to be snatched away from them at any moment. It broke my heart. We had to reassure them we had plenty of food.

That night, Donna tried to give Tyler a bath. But when she put water on his head, he screamed—a shriek of agonizing terror. Apparently, in the past, someone used to punish little Tyler by pouring hot water on him. Donna spoke to him quietly. "It's gonna be okay," she assured him.

Her thoughts went back to what she learned from her mama. *If anything will take you through, love will.* And a verse came to mind. It was John 4:18, "Perfect love drives out fear."

Donna started clinging to a hope that if she kept loving Tyler, she could help him overcome his fear. Over time, she built up his confidence to the point where he could trust her to pour warm water on his head. Her love came through for him. And Tyler's fear was gone. It was an important principle that she used to help her other kids conquer their own fears.

At our church Diann's new son, Nino, had been tugging on people's hearts. They said, "He doesn't even look like he's adopted! Who would want to give up this little boy?"

When we took Tyler and Mercedes to church for the first time, Donna had them all dressed up in their "Sunday-go-to-meetin'" clothes. There was five-year-old Mercedes with her beautiful curly hair and her pretty little-girl dress; and there was handsome two-year-old Tyler in his little suit and tie.

People grouped all around us and these two beautiful kids. Just like Nino before them, Tyler and Mercedes stole many hearts that day. We were peppered with questions and comments: "Where did you get these adorable children? We want to do what you're doing! How can we adopt?"

"These kids look cute," Donna and I told them, "but they've got baggage. They need somebody who will be there for them, unconditionally."

They listened to us. But the challenges didn't seem to matter.

They picked up Tyler and Mercedes and hugged them as if they were their very own.

God was at work. He was using Nino, Tyler, and Mercedes to tug at hearts—to rescue *more* kids out there. It was the beginning of something. And God saw it was good.

DOES LOVE CONQUER ALL?

But it wasn't long before we noticed things around the house were missing. Cookies, sodas, Vienna sausages, crackers. One morning Donna and I looked and looked all through the house. Finally, under Mercedes' bed, I discovered the missing food. Much of it was stale, some of it was moldy. We figured out that Mercedes was getting up late at night, taking the food, and hiding it under her bed. She was determined not to be hungry anymore.

Mercedes had been taught to steal by her biological mother. She'd go into stores and sneak food into pockets and purses. It's how she fed her brother. She didn't know any better.

I felt sorry for them, but I couldn't let them have their own way. They needed discipline, although with kids like these, spanking and raising your voice could be traumatic to them. It was tough work. Donna used every parenting skill that her mama taught her, but this was something new. These kids were different. The hardest part was helping them develop a healthy attitude and mind-set. We had to tell them again and again, "God loves you. You *are* somebody."

It was tough going. We'd help them overcome a hurdle, and then a few weeks later we'd face the same challenge all over again. We'd tell them to do homework or chores after school. They'd finally get it and do them a few days in a row. Success! Then a little while later they'd slip back into playing right after school. Failure!

They finally understood they didn't have to hide food under their beds anymore. Success! A few weeks later, we'd find food under their beds. Failure!

Donna would ask, "How was your day at school?" "Fine!" they'd say. Then she'd look through a backpack and find a note from the teacher about how they had misbehaved that day. Donna would confront them about it. And they would lie.

It was exhausting. But it wasn't just the kids. Many folks around town began questioning whether we were doing the right thing by adopting. Then, as if to prove their point, our kids would act out in school, and we'd hear about it from several sources.

Even though Donna had amazing perseverance, there were times when she wasn't sure if she could make it. She took it all personally. Sometimes she'd go to bed and just cry and pray. Despite my reassurance, Donna felt she was a failure as a mother. Many times she would lie awake at night and weep.

But the Lord would whisper back to her, *You're doing my will.* And she'd remember the first word He gave her: *Give back.*

Finally, in her own words, she had to "lose herself." She had to lose her worry about what other people thought. She had to lose her fear about not making it. She knew that God had led her on this path and that He hadn't stopped—He was leading her step by step each day. The same legacy He gave Donna's mother He was now giving to her.

Along the way, God used the kids to teach Donna new levels of patience. And she learned how to individualize her parenting, based on the needs of each child.

The challenges we faced from parenting and the community caused me to plunge deeper into God's Word and come up with all kinds of sermon material. Every day we were living out the trials of perseverance and the conquering power of love.

One day, Donna got a call from Mercedes' first-grade teacher. The teacher liked to give out candy to reward the kids at the end of the day. Now, the entire jar was missing. She found it in Mercedes' backpack.

Donna confronted Mercedes. "Did you take that candy?" Mercedes looked her straight in the eye and said, "No, ma'am."

Traditional discipline wasn't working for Donna. But one day God showed her a new approach—to get down on Mercedes' level and relate to her world. "The only way to get truth out of Mercedes was for me to become the kid."

She sat Mercedes down and talked with her. "My mother always expected me to tell the truth," she explained. "But my life was different from yours. I understand the reasons you would steal. If you're hungry and no one provides for you, I can understand. But you don't have to do that anymore. Your dad and I are providing for you. We aren't going to leave you."

Mercedes was insistent. "Mom, I didn't do it. I promise you."

"Okay, Mercedes, I'm your friend. And friends have to tell each other the truth so that friends are able to protect each other. I know we're mother and daughter, but right now, can we just play this little game, 'Just be friends'?

"I'm gonna be the little girl. And my mama has just asked me to tell the truth." And then something happened I hadn't planned. I began to cry. Mercedes held me. "Mama, don't cry." And she began to cry. Then she said, "Mama? I did it. I did it!"

The change didn't happen overnight. But gradually we began to see something take hold in our kids—a transformation. There was a gleam in their eyes that wasn't there before. They now believed us. They now knew—from deep inside—that they were loved and that we would never leave them.

It was still a tug of war with their old way of thinking. At times, we could see our love was winning them over. Other times, there were setbacks. As a pastor, I'm used to setbacks now and then. But one Sunday I got some bad news that hit me hard and hit me close. Someone had stolen the Sunday-school money from church.

It was Mercedes.

Three

"I'm Your Mama Now"

"Mercedes, where did this money come from?" I held up a little tin box. It was heavy, and it rattled with noise of several quarters.

"My friend gave it to me."

I knew it was a lie. And it stabbed me. My own little girl not only stole, but she looked straight into her daddy's eyes and lied. "Mercedes, I know you're lying to me. Where did you get this money?"

She insisted her friend gave it to her. I called her friend. But I already knew the answer. She had never given Mercedes any money.

Finally, Mercedes knew she was cornered. "Daddy," she said, "I'm not going to steal anymore."

I told her no one would trust her because she was stealing and lying. It would only hurt her. I told her God Himself would discipline her if she didn't straighten up. But nothing seemed to get through to her. She kept on stealing. Until the day we went to a local pancake house.

Circular stacks of hot brown pancakes and square stacks of steaming golden waffles had just arrived at our table, along with strawberries, whipped cream, and a generous complement of warmed-up maple syrup. The kids were eager to dig in. Suddenly, a police officer burst into the restaurant. Not just any police officer. This one was six foot six and weighed over three hundred pounds.

His authoritative voice filled the restaurant. "Who is Mercedes?!" Forks dropped on plates all around us. It was like one of those Western movies where the big guy walks into the saloon and the piano player suddenly stops playing. Everything was suspended.

The officer peered around the room like a searchlight. When that searchlight turned in our direction, Mercedes was like an ice statue. "I . . . I didn't do nothin!'" she managed to stutter. In a moment, the shadow of the giant-in-blue fell across our table. He looked straight at Mercedes with unblinking eyes. "If you steal again, I'm gonna lock you up in the jail. You understand?"

Somehow, Mercedes managed to nod. "Yes, sir."

My friend, the police officer, had made exactly the impression I had asked him to. No, the stealing didn't stop completely after that, but it did slow down considerably. The policeman at the pancake house helped mark a significant turning point for my little girl.

LISTENING FROM THE HEART

Diann Sparks, Donna's sister, had an emotional experience that changed her parenting perspective. Listen as she tells it:

There was another little girl—five years old—who lay in her bed at night, clutching a small rag doll named Molly. All her life, this little girl had been taken from one foster home to another foster home, from one bedroom to another bedroom, from one set of foster parents to another set of foster parents.

But Molly was always there for her. Molly's smudged face always smiled. Molly's eyes were always bright.

The little girl's own eyes were wide open. She thought about her pink bike, leaning against the garage door outside. Her foster mother got it last week from a garage sale. The handlebars were scratched up, the paint was fading, and the chain was a little rusty. But this bike was hers. The very first bike she ever had. And it was just like a big-girl bike, too, except for the training wheels.

She would ride and ride around in a circle in her neighborhood with Molly sitting in the little white basket that hung from the handlebars. She'd prop Molly up so she could see. And off they'd go!

The little girl loved to breathe in the smell of the sweet honeysuckle bushes as she rushed by. And when she biked up the steep hill, she loved to pretend that she was going to ride her bike right up into the sky!

The little girl wanted so badly to ride her bike one last time. But she had forgotten to put the lid on the milk. Her foster mother got mad. The little girl was grounded and sent to bed.

A strange light suddenly flooded her room through the window, moved across the ceiling, and stopped. She held Molly tighter. She heard the sound of a car idling right outside the window. The light faded. In the dark shadows of her room, she heard a car door open and slam. Footsteps on concrete.

Suddenly, the ceiling light blasted on. The little girl held Molly over her face to shield her eyes from the light. A drawer opened. She peeked between the strands of Molly's yellow yarn hair. Her foster mother was pulling out the little girl's clothes, and it looked like she was in a hurry. She glanced back at the little girl.

"Well, get up! Come on!" Everything was in a rush. A nice-smelling lady took the little girl's paper bag of clothes. The foster mother gave the little girl a quick hug and said good-bye.

The nice-smelling lady opened the car door for her and buckled her into a car seat. The little girl strained to look out the back window, but she was too short. The car started, and she pressed her nose against the window. The car was taking her away to another home, somewhere else, who knew where. She didn't really care anymore.

As the car turned, she peered through the window at the front yard. She strained to look. And there it was! Her pink bike, leaning against the garage door.

She had thought about asking her foster mother one more time if she could take it with her. But the foster mother had already said no, and the little girl didn't want to make her angry again. The bike would stay behind.

The little girl watched as long as she could. The bike got smaller and smaller behind her. Then a bush got in the way. And that was the last she ever saw it. She looked down at Molly, smiling at her. And she held Molly close. Molly's face became damp with real little-girl tears.

And in the middle of a small group of people, a young woman was crying.

The young woman was Diann. As part of Donna and Diann's adoption class, the social worker had asked Diann to role-play a real-life scenario—a little girl being taken from her home in the middle of the night.

As Diann had become the little girl, something changed in her heart. She thought about all the children in the foster-care system who were constantly shuffled from house to house, just like this. And it refreshed her whole outlook.

"Where I came from, my parents always showed us love," she said. "We didn't have very much, but we had love—a mama and a daddy who did what they could for us. But these children didn't have anybody."

As I mentioned earlier, when Diann signed up for these classes, she did it to support her sister. She didn't have any intention of actually adopting. But this night changed her.

NINO

In October 1997 Diann said yes to little four-year-old Nino. On the drive home, she looked in the rearview mirror. It was hard to believe she now had a son! It was even harder to believe how his mother gave birth to this beautiful boy and just left him behind at the hospital. Nino was now a handsome little boy with big eyes and long, thick eyelashes.

He was also unusually quiet. Now and then Diann glanced in her rearview mirror as Nino lay in the back seat. He never said a word. He never cried.

It turned out Nino was sick. His temperature was up. He said his head hurt. And he started throwing up. Diann rushed him to the emergency room.

Nino was suffering from severe allergies as well as asthma. The doctor prescribed some medicine for him and sent him home. Nino didn't like the taste of the medicine. But when Diann assured him it would make him feel better, he took it.

For days Nino's eyes were watery, his sinuses stuffed. Most of the time, he just lay quietly in his bed or on the sofa. When Diann took him to his first Sunday at church, he settled down in the pew next to her.

Over the following weeks, Diann cared for Nino, feeding him good meals, giving him his medicine along with plenty of water and juice. Gradually, Diann nursed the little boy back to health. Things started to go well.

Diann's sister Brenda got him his first pair of Nike tennis shoes, the exact kind he'd always wanted, in the exact color he'd always wanted—black. He clung to those shoes like they were a pair of teddy bears.

Diann had never seen him cry. But one evening, she peeked into Nino's bedroom and saw tears streaming down his cheeks. "What's wrong?" she asked. He choked up. "I wanna go back home," he said.

She stood there for a moment. With all she could muster from within, she said with a warm but confident love, "I'm your mama now." He didn't say anything. She hugged Nino and told him it would be okay. As time went on, he came to understand. And he came to know her as his "Mama."

One day, sometime later, he looked up at Diann with his little brows frowning. "Mama," he said, "why did you wait so long to come and get me?"

Tears filled her eyes. "Well," she answered, "it took me all that time to find you." And she picked him up and just held him.

Over time, Nino started to ask for a playmate, one who could live with them. It wasn't long after that when Susan Ramsey called from Child Protective Services (CPS). CPS had to go in and pull two boys out of a home fast, Susan said. She didn't say why. But she needed a home for them. Would Diann consider it?

All Diann could say was, "Wow." But she told Susan to go ahead and bring them on. Joshua was six years old. His brother, Randy, was five.

She loved all three boys. But it was too much for her. She wound up in the hospital for over a week, stressed out with a thyroid condition. She really didn't want the boys to go, and she didn't want Randy to be separated from his brother.

Donna noticed that Josh enjoyed staying over at our house. So she offered to have Josh live with us. That way, it would relieve the stress on Diann, and the brothers could still be in the same community. And you know, it worked out just right.

A LIVING SERMON

A preacher draws sermons from life around him. And with two adopted kids in our family—now three with Joshua—I had plenty of material! I started to preach on adoption at Bennett Chapel. "God commands us to take care of the orphans," I told the members. I didn't sugarcoat the prospect. It was a tough assignment to raise kids like these. Then again, it was more rewarding than we could have ever dreamed.

The people had fallen in love with Diann's adopted kids, Nino and Randy, and our kids—Tyler, Mercedes, and Josh. They looked at these children and couldn't believe the stories of how moms and dads had rejected and abused them.

The idea of reaching out to orphans was no longer a far-off notion. These were orphaned kids sitting right beside them in the pews. Beautiful kids. Well-behaved kids (after some work!).

I could tell something was stirring among the people in my congregation. But little did I know this stirring would revolution-ize our community.

People started asking questions. Some were getting a nudge from God. I told them about the adoption classes. But the classes required a 120-mile round-trip for 13 weeks. This was too much of a burden on our folks, many of whom were poor.

I asked Child Protective Services to give us some help. What if they held their classes here in Possum Trot? Sorry, said CPS. They required at least 10 families to start such a class. I said all right, then.

At our first meeting, we didn't have 10 families. We had 23! CPS was shocked. God was at work. The miracle that started with Donna and me and then Diann was now spreading . . . Donna and Diann's brother-in-law was among the new "converts."

KENDRIC

Calvin Williams's eyes and heart were glued to the television. It was one of those *Feed the Children* programs that show little children growing up with no mom or dad to watch over them and little or no food to eat. "Oh Lord, I wish I had one of those kids," Calvin whispered.

His wife, Jewel, overheard him. Calvin and Jewel had already raised two girls. Although Calvin loved his daughters dearly, something in him longed for a son.

It was a big event when Diann's new son, Nino, first arrived in Possum Trot. Nino wasn't just a new kid in the neighborhood; he was the new nephew in the family.

Nino was a handsome boy, intelligent, and well-mannered. "He'd say 'yes, ma'am' and 'no ma'am'; he'd do what you asked, and he enjoyed being around us," says Calvin.

"Diann, you've got a beautiful son," Jewel said.

"This is my boy," Diann said proudly. She looked at her sister with a twinkle in her eye. "You can't have my boy," she teased. "You'll have to get you one of your own."

Jewel looked at Calvin. As things stood now, they were about to become empty nesters—a sad time but a time of freedom as well. She had been looking forward to the freedom part. What they were contemplating would be like starting all over. She caught Calvin's eye. And she knew his heart. "If that's what you want to do," she said.

Their two daughters were very supportive. "You go for it," they said. "You'll be good for him."

Calvin wasted no time. He called Susan Ramsey. "Find one like Nino," he said.

Susan brought over pictures of kids available for adoption. And that was the first time they saw Kendric. The cute little five-year-old looked up at them from the page, smiling.

"I believe he's the one," Jewel said. Calvin agreed. They didn't need to look any further.

Calvin and Jewel knew from the stories they'd been told that Kendric would most likely have trouble adjusting. He might tear up the house, have eating disorders, lie, cheat, or steal. They weren't sure what to expect. All they knew was that God was leading them this way.

They drove to the foster home. And there they met the little boy who had smiled at them from the photo. The foster mom told Kendric, "This is gonna be your mama and daddy now."

"Okay," was all Kendric said. And he went back to playing with the other kids.

Calvin and Jewel took Kendric out to eat. He was polite. Rather shy. What was it like for a little boy to meet yet another couple who said they would be his mom and dad? Kendric had no idea Calvin and Jewel planned to be the parents who would stay, that they were in this forever.

"Next go-round, we'll come get you to stay with us," they told him.

"Okay." That's all he said.

When they showed up later to take Kendric home, he was ready.

"Okay."

Jewel fixed a meal for the family and they all sat down. Kendric stood by, waiting.

"C'mon and eat," she encouraged him. "We're all fixin' to eat around the table."

He stood there.

"C'mon," she coaxed. "Everything's all right."

Kendric took a step, then another. He quietly sat down at the table. But he didn't eat much at his first meal.

Calvin and Jewel took Kendric to church on Sunday, and their new son quickly became the center of attention. Everybody

gathered around, fussing over him, cooing over him, smiling at him. Kendric snuggled close to his new mama and daddy.

"He looks like one of you!" a few of them remarked. And they were right. He looked just like Jewel's brother Kerry. Already, Kendric was fitting in.

For the first couple of weeks, Kendric remained shy at church. "He stuck close to us," says Jewel. "But it wasn't long before he got unstuck. His shy didn't hold long," she says with a chuckle. Kendric quickly warmed up to the people around him. "We couldn't shut him up after that."

Kendric's arrival changed things a lot at home. After years of having older kids in the house, Calvin and Jewel now had a little young one to take care of. They had to show him how to put his clothes on, how to brush his teeth, how to take care of himself.

As they prayed over Kendric, they found God's encouragement. *This is the one you asked for,* they felt Him say. *You are blessed with him. Help him, train him, teach him about Me and about life.*

Jewel thought back to her own mother, who would take children in from all around Possum Trot and feed them. Her mama didn't care who they were. She would treat them all with the same love and care, as if they were her own.

Now, in a small way, Jewel was doing the same, and there were little rewards along the way. When she bought something for Kendric, he was genuinely grateful. "Thank you, Mom," he'd say. "I love you."

He came home from school one day very excited. "I gotta surprise for you!" he said proudly. "But you'll have to wait till Mother's Day." When the day arrived, he rushed to his room, where he had hidden his special gift. He came back and handed it to Jewel.

It was a little cardboard box with flowers on it that he had made just for her. She opened up the box and found a little seed to plant.

He stood there and beamed.

Jewel hugged her little son and gave him a kiss. She planted the seed in a container. Over time, it grew into a healthy little plant.

Calvin enjoyed having a son. He took Kendric to basketball games and football games. As Kendric got older, Calvin taught him to take care of the yard—mowing, raking, cleaning up.

Kendric joined his school basketball team, and the coach put him in a game for a little while. "He was very excited," Calvin remembers. "He was jumping up and down!"

Calvin has had "man to man" talks with Kendric over the years, preparing his son for the things he'll be facing ahead. Calvin felt it was especially important to teach Kendric respect—respect for elders, for young ladies.

When Kendric had first arrived, it was like starting over for Calvin and Jewel. But God was also teaching them through Kendric. "God taught me to give more love toward people," Calvin says. "Any time you can reach out and take someone else's

child into your home, that's got to be love. That's what God is all about," he adds. "He's about love."

Kendric made a smooth transition in his new home. But that's not always the case—as you'll see when you meet Terri.

Four

Finally Home

In 1999 God nudged us to adopt another girl—a light-skinned African American named Terri. She was nine years old.

When it comes to adoption, most kids this age are passed over. That's because in an abusive environment, the older the kids get, the more messed up they get. And Terri was one messed-up little girl. She had been in 10 other families. Ours was number 11.

When we got her, Terri was convinced she was a cat. And this wasn't just a game of pretend. Her previous foster mother left Terri all alone for long stretches of time. Terri ate and slept with her only real companion—a tomcat. Over time, she adopted the mannerisms and habits of her furry friend.

Terri had been taken to a psychiatrist—she went through professional therapy—but she still insisted she was a cat.

When it was time to bring Terri home with us, she jumped

into the back of the car and drew herself up, just like a cat. "What is wrong with you, girl?" I asked her. "I'm a cat," she replied.

When we brought her home, she stayed outside. I went out to get her. She jumped up on the table on all fours. "I'm a cat," she said.

"You're not a cat," I replied.

"Yes I am," she insisted.

"A cat has hair all over. You don't." Her own hair was knotted and kinky.

"I'm a cat," she repeated. "I've got four legs."

"No you're not," I responded. Then the light went on for me.

"If you're a cat, you can't come into my house, 'cause cats around here stay outside. If you're a cat, you'll have to stay outside and eat cat food and raw liver and gizzards, just like real cats." She thought about this for a while.

"That's what a cat eats," I said, "and that's what I'll feed you."

She thought about it some more. Then she replied, "I don't think I want to be a cat anymore." She came on inside, and that was the end of the cat.

I didn't find Terri's cat problem in the index of a child-raising book. This was far beyond me. It was far beyond the experts. I had to rely on God to show me what to do. And He did. But little did I know the cat problem was only the beginning.

Terri is now 16 years old and speaks with such a soft, sweet voice you'd never guess what a brutal experience she had as a little one. This is her story.

TERRI'S STORY

I think my mother was insane.

Many days, she'd come home with a black eye. Blood on her clothes. She'd get beaten up. And she'd beat me. I'd run across the street to my grandmother's to stay with her. And my mother would come over, take me out of the house, and beat me with a broom. Other times, she'd force me to drink alcohol and smoke cigarettes.

One time when I was about three years old, she had me stay with one of her boyfriends, who happened to be married. I don't remember his name, but the lady's name was Peaches. Peaches would hit me, and I tried to fight back with my hands. One time, she tossed me up on the kitchen counter. I reached up and grabbed anything I could find—salt, pepper, hot sauce—and threw it at her. I got some in her eyes and ran away.

But Peaches and her husband got me. And they punished me in the worst way they could think of. They raped me. Then they took a cigarette lighter and burned the skin on my legs—I still have the scars. After that, I passed out.

They laid me in a ditch. I was out of it. I guess they thought I was dead. I couldn't open my eyes. I was numb. They left me there.

When I woke up, it was dark. I was shocked. Shaking. Crying. I wanted my mama. The man and Peaches came and got me before daybreak and took me home.

My mother noticed I was upset. She thought I was just tired. But she noticed I was dirty. I went into the bathroom and cried. She tried to check on me, but I yelled, "Don't come near me! No! No! You can't come near me!"

Then she saw the burned spots on my legs. "What happened?" she asked. She started crying when she realized what actually did happen.

She took me to the hospital, and the medical staff saw I had been raped. They cleaned me up as best they could. When I got home, I couldn't sleep. It hurt if anything touched the burns on my legs.

My mother pressed charges. I had to testify in court about what happened. And the man and Peaches went to jail for what they did to me. They were out of my life for good.

But my mother was still with me.

Around this time I remember hearing my sister hollering in the next room. She was about 15. She kept hollering. And then the hollering stopped all of a sudden.

My mother came in the room where I was. She was crying and screaming, "My baby's dead! My baby's dead!" I found out later that she had suffocated my sister with a pillow.

It was awhile before she ended up in jail. Meantime, I don't understand why, but she kept beating me. One time it was so bad, I had to go back to the hospital again. My mother lied. She said I went into a closet and beat myself and bruised myself and cut myself. "She's just crazy," she told the people at the hospital. And she was the one who did it all.

My face was swollen. There were scratches on my face and whelps around my eyes. I remember they put me on medication every three or four hours just to calm my nerves. I stayed there for a long time.

Once in a while, my mother would come and see me at the hospital. But I'd never say anything to her. I was mad at her. She had beaten me and then lied.

I was taken from her and put in the foster system. Meantime, they locked up my mother for a while—11 or 12 years. She got out a few years ago. But I can't go anywhere near her. Legal reasons.

I still have pictures of my mother—four or five photos. Now and then, I stare at my mother in those pictures. And I ask her, "Why?"

At my first foster home, they acted like they cared. But their discipline was kind of harsh. It scared me.

Sometimes I had to go to the bathroom, and I would stare at the ceiling in the dark because I was too afraid to step out into the hall. Afraid someone would grab me and pull me into his room and do nasty things to me. I held on as best I could.

One night, I was ready. I had gotten a little bucket out of the kitchen. So whenever I needed to go at night, I'd just pee in the bucket and stick it under my bed. It worked. Until my foster parents found the bucket.

They were upset. They forced down my head and stuck my face in the bucket of pee.

After that, if they just looked at me wrong, I'd start shaking and sweating. Whenever they'd holler, I'd get scared and just pee on myself.

I went from foster home to foster home. When I was nine, I was brought here. Mama and Daddy were working in the garden. They met me at the door and made me feel welcome.

About a week and a half later, my caseworker showed up again.

He asked me how I liked the Martins. I told him it was fun here. "But I'm ready to go back home."

He looked at me. "This is going to be your final destination for now." I cried. I had moved so much. I didn't want to move again. I didn't want to have to get used to another family. Again. I was tired of the routine. At first, everyone's nice, everyone's happy. Then the caseworker leaves, and the house turns into another hell.

But the caseworker left this time and nothing bad happened After two or three days, I had to admit it: Something was different here. The love and the care stayed steady. Still, I didn't trust them. I couldn't let my guard down. I didn't want my hope to be smashed.

Sometime later, my sister and brother were chasing each other through the house, and they knew they weren't supposed to. Mom raised her voice and said, "You all better stop running through the house!"

I froze. All those old feelings came back to me. The betrayal. The fear. I broke down and begged Mom, "Please, don't talk to them like that!" I knew what was coming next. She was going to beat them up. I pleaded with my sister and brother, "Please don't do that anymore! I don't want you getting into trouble!"

Mom took me aside and sat me down. Was I in trouble now? She looked me in the eyes. "Terri," she said, "we don't beat our kids. We show them love. Now and then, we might have to raise our voice to our kids. But it's not to be mean. We're trying to get their attention, so they'll know they're doing wrong.

"But let me tell you something, Terri. You don't have to worry anymore about anybody beating you or beating the kids. I promise you, we won't do anything to hurt you kids because we love you."

Her words helped me feel a little more comfortable. But still, I wasn't sure. After a long time of watching her and how she treated me and the other kids, I gradually began to realize something important. My mom was telling me the truth. That was something new to me.

I had secretly hoped that maybe this time—unlike every other time—Mom and Dad weren't just pretending to love me. It was a tiny hope that had been beaten down many times before.

But as I saw over time, Mom and Dad weren't pretending. Their love was real. Their care was real. And my hope was real.

Finally . . . I was home.

Five

"You've Got To Be Out of Your Mind"

Just down the road from Donna's old homestead is a neatly kept double-wide with a huge front yard. Out back is a quiet pond with trees branching over it. This is the where Glen and Theresa Lathan live. And where a funny, amazing thing happened.

Just 30 minutes after Tyler and Mercedes came to live with us, my wife invited Theresa to come over to see them. Donna looked at Theresa and said, "You know, you're the ideal person to do this. You have a heart for children. You love them."

Theresa smiled. "I might." She was being nice.

She had no idea what was about to happen.

Theresa and Glen already had three children at home—two

11-year-old boys and a 7-year-old girl. Theresa was content with the size of her family. It seemed just right.

But Donna kept talking to her. And I started to preach on adoption, reminding folks that we're *all* adopted into the royal family of God. God told us to reach out to these orphans with His love.

Word got around that an adoption class was starting at the church. "I thought I might just go through with the class," she says now. Her heart had begun to open up. "I was thinking maybe we could adopt one more girl to go with the girl I had."

She talked to Glen. He wasn't sure this was something he wanted to do, but he agreed to go through the class with her.

THE FIVE SISTERS

One day when Theresa came home from work, there was a message on the answering machine from a social worker. Theresa called her.

"We were kinda talking at the office, and your name came up," the social worker said.

Theresa got excited. *Could this be the little girl?*

"We thought you'd be the perfect family."

Yes! This was the call! It was time!

"We have five sisters."

What?!

"They're separated, and they don't even know they're sisters."

Theresa's heart dropped. *Five sisters—and they don't even know one another exists?*

"Could you talk it over with your husband? And do you think we could possibly bring them over next weekend for a visit?"

Hmmm. Theresa had some convincing to do. Finally, she worked up enough gumption to approach the subject with Glen.

"The social worker called today," she said, trying her best to sound casual. Now for the tough part. She talked real fast so he couldn't interrupt her. "They've got five girls and they're separated and they don't even know one another. Can you imagine?"

Glen responded the way any normal father would.

"Five girls?! You gotta be out of your mind!"

"Well, we don't have to do it. But let the social workers bring them for a visit this weekend, and we'll see how everything goes."

"No way! Not five girls. That's just too many children. We already have three!"

"Glen, I've already okayed them to bring the girls for the weekend. I'm not trying to push you into anything. If you feel this is not what you want to do, then let's just keep them for the weekend, all right?"

Glen thought for a moment. He sighed. "All right," he said. "If you feel you can handle these girls for a weekend . . . then . . . let 'em come on."

It was Labor Day weekend. The five girls came on a Friday.

Eight-year-old Shereatha, six-year-old Shenequa, four-year-old Rashaundria, and two-and-a-half-year-old twins—Shameria and Tameria.

They were shy at first. This was the first time these sisters had all been together. But they took to Glen quickly as the father figure—the father they missed. They started jumping all around him. These girls desperately needed a daddy. Glen started melting.

Later that weekend, Glen looked at Theresa. "We gotta take them back Monday?" he said.

"That's what they told me."

His eyes locked with hers. A moment of silence. "If you feel you can handle it . . . if you think you can really take care of these girls and give them what they need, then . . . "

Was he really going to go for it? All five girls?

". . . we'll take 'em."

It was one of those pivotal moments where one thing is said and all life changes. And it was a good change.

But not for everyone. Their one "original" little girl at home—seven-year-old Miracle—wasn't happy. She was Daddy's girl—his only girl. Now she stood back in the shadows and watched the invaders come in and take her daddy's heart. Her mom's, too.

When the girls came to live with the family, Miracle referred to them as "those girls." It was a struggle for her. Up till then, she never had to share her room with anybody. But there were now ten people in a two-bedroom house. Miracle had to share.

For a year or so it was hard on her. But gradually, after some talks with Mama, Miracle began to warm up to a couple of the girls. Now and then, she started sharing little things—a toy, a doll. The girls knew Miracle hadn't been happy with their coming. But now they were surprised. They appreciated the special effort Miracle was making.

The Lathans were now a family. A family with eight children and a mom and dad who truly loved them.

This sounds like a warm and happy ending. But it's not. Oh no . . . it's just the beginning.

AND THREE MORE MAKE ELEVEN!

Across the street were Theresa's sister Mollie and her husband, Joe. They were also members of our church and heard the call to adopt. Mollie and Joe had decided to adopt three kids. Andre was now 12, Justin 11, and Lovey 9. Their mother had been a drug addict who never stopped her habit, even when she was carrying her children.

But now the kids didn't have to worry anymore about being shuffled around to yet another family. Mollie and Joe Brown were Mom and Dad and took good care of them.

In September 2003 Mollie died. The children, who had already been through so much trauma in their young lives, now lost the only "true" mother they had ever known.

Then the unthinkable happened—six months later Joe died.

The three children had now lost both parents. They were going to be sent back once more into foster care.

I can't do it, Theresa thought. She tried to get around it. And every time she would try to say "I can't do it," she could hear something saying, *Yes, you can.*

Yes, you can. She went over the numbers in her mind. "Eleven children. Eleven children! I can't do it!"

Yes, you can.

She knew what the kids had been through in their very young days. And now they were orphans again. It wasn't their fault.

Yes, you can.

Glen was having reservations of his own. But he didn't really see they had any other choice. "We didn't want them to go back to the system where they came from," he says. Besides, his brother-in-law had been like a brother to him. "I knew he'd want me to do the best I could for those kids."

Yes, you can.

Theresa sighed. "Well, Lord," she said, "if You just give me the strength to do it, I'll do it. Three more won't break us. We'll figure out something."

Glen had made up his mind as well. "Let them live with us."

Theresa gave up the life she thought she wanted to live. She gave up her job at the local flooring company where she had worked for 16 years. During that time, Glen and Theresa had also paid off their house. Now they gave up living debt free. They took out a mortgage to buy a larger mobile home to accommodate all the kids.

So they brought them in. Glen can chuckle about it all now. When they started with three kids, he couldn't imagine bringing in five more. Impossible! But they did. And now, three more!

The Lathans are now a family of 11 children. It's a squeeze in the mobile home. The kids have to share rooms. And a couple of beds are out where the living room would be. But they keep the house neat. And the Lathans have made it work.

Like Christmas, for instance. "We were so used to just three kids," Theresa says. "We could run out at the last minute and pick up something. But with all these kids now, we have to start way back in September!"

When Theresa thinks back to the first time Donna said, "You're the ideal person to do this," she never dreamed she'd end up with this many children.

People often ask her how she does it. "I don't know!" she says. "I don't really think about what I have to do. I just do it."

And she's learning along the way. "God has taught me to be patient. How to appreciate what I have. And how to love 'in spite of.' In spite of problems or difficulties my kids have, I keep love in front of all that."

She keeps her focus on one thought: *I'm not doing this for myself. I'm doing it to help somebody else.*

It's not a glamour story. It's ministry work. "You're taking in children who have been molested. Children who had to eat out of pots that rats were crawling in. Children who would eat like animals, down on the floor. You have to train them all over again as if they were one-year-olds. You've gotta be up at odd hours to attend to them when they're crying out in the night. And when you leave for the grocery store, you've gotta deal with their very real fear—a fear that you'll never come back, that you'll leave them all alone again."

But in the middle of all this, Glen and Theresa have discovered some great rewards. The reward of knowing they've done the right thing. The reward of knowing they've rescued these kids from abandonment and abuse. The reward of knowing the trust of little ones who give their mom and dad the biggest hugs they possibly can.

Glen says, "They don't have to worry anymore about where they're going to stay tonight. They don't have to worry about having food on the table or clothes on their backs. Now they have a place to stay and food to eat. They have a family."

The Cartwright sisters

Bishop Martin

TYLER MARTIN

Bishop and Donna Martin

Kendric Williams

The Lathan family

The Brown children

Johnnie Brown

Kerry Cartwright

Joshua Martin

JO BETH DAW

Bishop and Donna Martin with church

Terri Martin

Pineywoods   Outreach

SAVING A GENERATION

EPART

JUDY BOWMAN

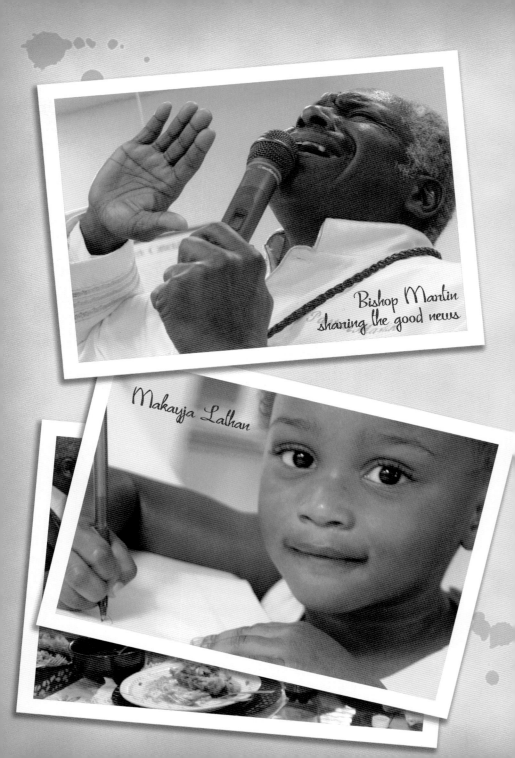

Bishop Martin
sharing the good news

Makayja Lathan

The Brown children worshiping

Terri and Princeton Martin

JOSHUA MARTIN

Nino Sparks

The late Susan Ramsey

MERCEDES MARTIN

Six

A No-Matter-What Perseverance

They pulled a sheet over her face . . . she was dead.

This is the story of Johnnie Brown, a grandmother who made a life-changing decision. You could also call it a death-defying decision.

Johnnie and her husband, Fred, were members of our church. When they heard me preach about adoption, they didn't just nod their heads. They examined their hearts.

A lot of parents coast in the empty-nest years, busying their lives with things they've been wanting to do. But Johnnie and Fred were different. The last one of their kids left home in 1993. Now it was 2000, Johnnie and Fred were in their 40s, and they were seriously considering becoming parents all over again with a new set of children.

A lot of folks called them crazy. A family member told Fred, "You need to get Johnnie's brain checked."

But they took a step forward anyway and decided to take the adoption class we had at our church. That's when they saw the photo. As they were leafing through pictures of all the little children who needed mommies and daddies, they paused when they came upon a photo of triplets. Two boys and a girl. Adorable. Precious.

Among their grandchildren, Johnnie and Fred already had two sets of twins. It got them thinking.

"Wouldn't that be nice?" they said to each other. "A set of triplets!" They learned that the triplets were two-and-a-half years old. Their names were Tevin, Terrance, and Tiayana. And they had a baby sister as well, who had been separated from them— 18-month-old Keiosha.

Johnnie and Fred looked at each other. They already knew. They were going to be a mommy and daddy again.

A ROUGH START

The triplets had already been in foster care for two years. And this was their fourth family! They had no structure, no boundaries whatsoever. Soon after the triplets and their little sister arrived at their new home, it was bedlam. They touched and tugged at everything, taking things down, throwing things around. They broke picture frames, destroyed miniblinds, and broke a picnic table. These little ones were weapons of mass destruction.

They were amazingly articulate, too, in a way you wouldn't expect. They all used foul language—even the 18-month-old! Little Keiosha was especially adept at cussing out her older siblings. When she got mad, she'd call them the worst imaginable things.

Johnnie was shocked. "Where do you get these words from?" she asked Keiosha. "I get them from my*self,*" she'd answer. Meantime, on his first day in his new home, two-and-a-half-year-old Tevin stood up to Johnnie like a little cowboy in Pampers, facing a duel. He looked up at her with his hands on his hips and an attitude to match. "Girl, if you don't get up and get me some ice cream . . ."

"Oh no," Johnnie said firmly. "I don't think so!"

Johnnie now had another challenge on her hands—four kids in diapers! Fred was a truck driver who was on the road a lot. So a lot of the child rearing (and taking care of children's rears) was left to Johnnie.

Nobody had taken time to potty train the kids. But she encouraged them. "You're gonna wear big-girl and big-boy underclothes. You're ready!" It made the kids proud to graduate from diapers. Johnnie had the triplets potty trained in two weeks.

Keiosha, though, was stubborn. She would stand defiantly in front of Johnnie and just go in her clothes, with a look on her face

that said, "Whatcha gonna do about it?" Whatever Johnnie told her to do, she would do the opposite.

And yet at the same time, ironically, Keiosha was very attached to Johnnie. Keiosha had been raised in a white family and was terrified of black people. When she first saw Johnnie and Fred, she almost went into a spasm. She wouldn't come to Johnnie for anything. She'd just cry.

But on the third visit, Johnnie says, it was like "divine intervention." The caseworker brought Keiosha to Johnnie. "Let me see if she'll come to you now."

Johnnie reached out her hand to her. "C'mon, baby. Let's c'mon to Mama."

And Keiosha stepped out on her little legs and wobbled over to Johnnie. And she clung to her newfound mother. From that day forward, Johnnie was Mama. This angry little girl became the sweetest little thing that ever happened to Johnnie.

A ROUGH MIDDLE

Johnnie had other interesting challenges. Without warning, the kids would just pull down their pants. These were wild children. For about a month Johnnie had to lock herself away in the house with these kids to try to get them straightened out before she could even bring them to church.

When the triplets turned three, Johnnie went out and got the biggest birthday cake she could find. She decorated the house with balloons and streamers and purchased a boatload of gifts. The kids were confused. They asked their dad, "Why is Mama doing all this?"

"She's decorating for your birthday!"

The kids frowned. Fred was curious.

"You mean, you never had a birthday party before?"

"No, sir. Never."

In all their shifting around from home to home, no one had ever taken time to celebrate their birthday. Johnnie and Fred had the privilege of being the very first to do so.

Then it was time for the triplets to go to prekindergarten. This would give Johnnie more focused time with Keiosha. The triplets all went to the same classroom, and they were so cute! The teachers would spoil them. They'd show off the triplets as they walked them around, the little girl in front and the two little boys on the side.

But Johnnie knew things would change once the teachers crossed their wills. She warned them not to spoil the kids. "They'll show you a thing or two," she said under her breath.

Then the calls started. Teachers would call Johnnie every day, sometimes three and four times a day. The kids were terrorizing the classroom. They had temper tantrums. They would fight the kids and bite the teachers. One triplet got a healthy chunk of teacher—the teacher was bitten so badly she had to get a tetanus shot. Tevin kicked another teacher in the knee. "Look at my knee!" the teacher showed Johnnie. It was swollen from the impact. She even had to go to the doctor.

Johnnie figured out the triplets' strategy. They were determined to be so awfully bad that they would be sent home to be where Mama was. But Johnnie knew they had to learn. "You're gonna stay," she'd tell them. And eventually, they caught on that she meant what she said.

At home the kids would follow her every move. She'd be cooking in the kitchen, look down, and see four little faces looking up at her. Other times, she'd turn around and almost fall over the little parade of kids behind her. She would wake up in the middle of the night and find these little kids, sitting quietly side by side, watching over her.

Finally Johnnie asked, "Why are you all following me like this?"

"We're scared you're gonna leave us," they replied.

"I'm not gonna leave you," she said.

She knew she couldn't. Nobody would keep kids as wild as these. She had to do it. But there was a deeper reason. The vow.

THE VOW

Johnnie and Fred had made a vow that they would not take a chance on the kids' going back to the earthly hell that had shaped them and threatened to draw them into its clutches again. It was the hell that Johnnie and Fred were determined to conquer.

They came across documents that unraveled the story of that hell. The kids' mother would never stay in one place more than a few months. She was in and out of jail. She'd leave the babies locked up in a house with their five-year-old brother—a house infested with rats and roaches. He'd try to take care of the babies as best he could, as they crawled around on the floor. He'd go off to the store and steal something for them to eat.

The babies developed bad diaper rashes. They came down with bronchitis and suffered from asthma. Their skin became severely dry and scaly. Keiosha developed an iron deficiency.

And these were just the documented traumas the kids went through. There were signs of worse abuse. It was no wonder they acted out the way they did.

And so Johnnie and Fred made the vow. They knew God had given them this special assignment and along with it a special love. They were determined that these kids—*their* kids—would never face hell again.

Many times their vow was tested. Many times Johnnie was tempted to call Child Protective Services and say, "You need to come get 'em. I can't deal with them anymore. It's just too much on me."

But she persevered. "I had to resolve that I could endure better than they could," she would say later. "I didn't want to throw them away." She and Fred stuck with them.

Johnnie's perseverance would cost her. She had been injured in a car accident soon after getting the kids, which left her in a lot of pain. With the stress of raising the kids and dealing with the pain, she began to experience severe health problems. She

went from taking no medication at all to carrying around gallon-size bags of meds, just to function through the day. Over time, she developed fibromyalgia, asthma, diabetes, and high blood pressure.

Tevin and Terrance would come home from school and see their mama in pain. "Mama, how are you feeling?" they'd ask her.

"I feel okay." She lied. She never wanted them to know that they had anything to do with her stress.

"Well, your eyes don't look good. Do you need a banana?" They knew she ate lots of fruits and vegetables to try to keep healthy.

But it wasn't working. Johnnie became severely dehydrated. Over time she lost 50 pounds. On Easter weekend, Fred took her to the hospital.

And that's when Johnnie died.

ON EASTER SUNDAY

"Charge!"

The defibrillator was ready.

"Clear!"

The doctor pressed the paddles on the lifeless body of Johnnie Brown. Three hundred joules of electricity surged through the paddles. Johnnie's body jerked upward in an unnatural arch, then sunk down on the bed.

The nurse checked the reading. "Still on defib." The line on the EKG was virtually flat. The doctor tried again. And again. Nothing.

Johnnie had been gone for 20 minutes. The doctor had done everything he could. But Johnnie's husband had the same kind of perseverance she had. Fred wouldn't let them stop trying.

Finally though, reality was sinking in. "Mr. Brown," the doctor said, "I'm sorry. Her veins have collapsed. Nothing is flowing through her body. All signs of brain activity are gone. Even if we could bring her back right now, she wouldn't be able to walk or talk. She wouldn't even know she was in this room."

Fred shook his head. The nurse pulled the sheet up to cover Johnnie's face. "One more time," Fred said. "One more time."

"Mr. Brown, I'm sorry. It's no use." The doctors had done everything they could. Fred had done everything he could. It felt as though he could finally stop holding his breath. A wave of emotions slammed into him.

That's when a nurse noticed something unusual. Ever so slightly, Johnnie's foot moved. The doctor saw it.

Meanwhile Johnnie was enjoying a sensation of rest she had never known before.

"All I knew was that I was in a peaceful place. And no pain! For the first time in six years."

"She's on sinus tach [fast heartbeat] at 130!"

"It felt like I was in suspended animation. Just floating."

"Charge!"

"It was the best peace and comfort I had ever felt in my entire life."

"Clear!"

"Something hit my body. It felt as if a slab of concrete slammed into me."

"Pressure reading forty over thirty!"

"I woke up. There were all kinds of wires and everything hooked up to me. And that's when the pain came back. Excruciating pain. My body went into spasms. They said my blood sugar was so high, my blood had turned to syrup. They kept asking my name and where I lived and what my telephone number was. And I told them. The doctors were baffled. They couldn't believe it."

"I don't understand why you're still living," one doctor said. "I don't understand why you're not in a morgue."

Johnnie had suffered a stroke. But it was clear that a miracle was in the making. On Easter Sunday, no less.

She stayed in the intensive care unit for five days. She was totally blind for two months. Gradually, her sight returned. The pain was still there. But Johnnie Brown was alive.

"Look at me," she says today. "It's Jesus. It's a miracle."

A HAPPY ENDING

When she came home, the kids doted on her. "Mama, you okay?" Tevin asked. "What do you want me to do for you?" He did whatever he could to make her feel comfortable. And he'd tell the other children, "Mama's sick now, so you all need to do your part to help out."

The kids helped out. Gave her lots of hugs. Told her over and over how much they loved her.

In a quiet moment, Tevin confided in her, "Mama, I don't know what I would have done if you had died. I would have gone right behind you because you're my everything."

"Baby, no," Johnnie said. "I cannot have you saying this. I want you to feel that way about Jesus. He needs to be your everything. Trust in Him. I didn't come here to stay. I've got an appointed time to die. I don't know when it's going to be, but you've got to be able to handle it, whenever it comes. We've all gotta go, Tevin. We just don't know when."

"I know, Mama," he said, "but who would take care of me? You're the best mama I ever had."

Today, Johnnie Brown is still in pain. But there's a comfort in knowing she has invested well in four little children—Tevin, Terrance, Tiayana, and Keiosha. It's amazing to note the transformation. These kids are now some of the most well-mannered, well-behaved kids in all of Possum Trot. They're genuinely good kids.

"I know it wasn't me," says Johnnie. "It was Jesus." The same Jesus who did the miracle of raising Johnnie from the dead did the miracle of raising her children. And He used Johnnie and Fred as His miracle workers.

When Johnnie gets frustrated, Tevin encourages her and prays for her. "God's gonna bless you, Mama." Johnnie looks at her four children, and she knows . . . God already has.

Seven

The View from Outside Possum Trot

You probably figured out by now that I don't sugarcoat things. Adoptions don't always turn out to be days of Hallmark-card moments. And the challenges we faced weren't just inside our homes. All kinds of talk circulated around us.

"Those folks are crazy."

"Yep, they've lost their minds."

"They don't have any business doing this."

"You're right. They don't know what they're doing."

"How could they bring kids like that into their homes?"

"They're adopting for money; that's what it is."

We certainly didn't go through all this for money. Yes, we got assistance from the state, and we were grateful. But when we moved from being foster parents to adoptive parents, the assistance dropped significantly.

Before we adopted, we were able to make ends meet. Now, we had more clothes to buy. More laundry every day. And we had to get a bigger car. At times, things got really tight. Asking God to provide became a daily prayer. We had to become wise shoppers and catch all the sales.

No, this wasn't about money. This was about true treasure, far beyond what money could buy.

We didn't consider these children foster kids or adopted kids. We considered them *our* kids. We loved them as our own, because they *were* our own. And we discovered great rewards— eternal rewards and earthly rewards. That's because we didn't adopt for our own gratification. We did this for the kids. And when you reach out to one of these forgotten ones, God smiles.

NEVER GIVE UP

It's interesting what happens when you start really partnering with God—doing what makes Him smile. You start thinking as He does. Big. Really big. As we got more and more kids, a dream started to form in my mind—a dream of a recreation center for these kids, a place where they could run and jump and play, a place where they could have fun.

We looked at adding on to the church. That didn't work out.

We got loads of promises—people and agencies said they were going to help out. They didn't. I kept making phone calls, knocking on doors. It was going to take probably a million dollars to build something like this. Where were we going to get that kind of money? The average income in our community was under thirty thousand dollars a year.

But that didn't matter. I could see the building in my mind. This was a God-sized dream. And whatever it took, it was worth it for our kids. It was worth pressing through the challenges, the negative talk, and the broken promises.

Perseverance is part of our culture in Possum Trot. It's something God has forged in us through the tough stuff of life. Over the years, He's taught us that we can trust Him—that He'll be there to carry us through, no matter what we face. This kind of God-given perseverance causes people to take note.

"I've been in adoption all my career—over 30 years," says Judy Bowman, regional director for Child Protective Services, "and this is the first time I've ever seen anything like this." She explains, "A lot of people show interest in adoption but never follow through. These people did. They all pitched in."

For comparison, Judy says in all 15 counties of her region, people adopted 74 kids in 2005. In a little over three years, the small community of Possum Trot adopted some 70 kids.

Judy worked with Susan Ramsey, our caseworker. At first their office was a bit leery—could our community handle the toughest kids in foster care? And on our side, there was a traditional distrust of the system. Susan was the bridge. She believed in us, and we trusted her. She guided us through.

Susan wasn't just a caseworker; she was like an angel. As we look back now, we know she was commissioned for this work. She wouldn't just place a child with somebody who was willing. She took time to match the child's needs with the best parents possible for that child. Then she'd spend countless hours helping families get ready for adoption—educating them, answering their questions, making sure they were prepared for the transition. In the process, she became just like family to the people of Possum Trot. When Susan became sick with cancer, the community rallied around her as if she was one of our own. That's because she *was*. We had adopted *her!*

Many adoptions end up in what's called "disillusionment." It just doesn't work out. But as Judy said—in addition to God's grace and Susan's care—our people made good on their commitments. Here's proof: *Not one adopted child has gone back into the system!* That's not only remarkable; it's a miracle.

"They don't throw away people," says Judy. "If somebody in the community is going through a rough time, they keep the hurting person in the fold."

Judy's right. Our community pitches in. It's like one big extended family where there's a personal interest in one another's kids. If parents are having trouble with their children, or if they're facing a crisis of some sort, folks from the community will go over to their house to talk with the family and pray for them.

When Johnnie Brown got so sick she wasn't able to take care of her children, we took food over to her house and prayed for her. We did chores around the house. Then we took her four little ones and watched them for a day or so.

In Possum Trot you can't tell who's adopted and who's not. That's because we don't make a distinction between the adopted kids and the others. We're all family.

SUSAN RAMSEY

The caseworkers were amazed at this big, bold experiment in Possum Trot. They were amazed with our people.

"The Browns got the triplets plus one," Judy recalls. "I remember Susan coming back from their house. Those kids were really wild. She said she didn't stay very long. She was afraid they would change their minds and give the kids back!"

Things are a lot different now, according to Judy. "That family has done a wonderful job. The kids are beautiful, smart, and well-behaved."

Susan Ramsey had been our caseworker from the beginning, a virtual saint in our community. As Susan got sicker with the cancer, we all felt her pain. She wanted us to be close to her. So we visited her in her home, and we held her hand.

One Sunday morning while we were getting ready for church, the phone rang. Donna felt something drop in her spirit, even

before anybody picked up the phone. It was Judy. "Donna, we lost Susan."

We were devastated. Susan had been the one to get us started. She had believed in us. She was one of us. A large group of our church members showed up at her memorial service.

When Susan died, she left a void. Her best friend, JoBeth Daw, took over for her. She had heard about the people of Possum Trot. But now she got to work with us directly. And she was amazed at our commitment.

"They have such a strong support system within the church. They come from big families," JoBeth says "They raise children, and they're good at it! There's lots of love, lots of commitment. And if there's a problem with a child, it's a community problem."

That's because we don't just watch out for our own children. We watch out for all the Possum Trot children.

JoBeth adds, "You don't have to have a degree to have family values. And you don't have to have a higher education to be qualified as a good parent."

Actually, by adopting these kids, we *did* get a higher education. Education from God Himself!

THE WORLD TAKES A LOOK AT POSSUM TROT

The folks at Child Protective Services weren't the only ones who were amazed at what was happening in Possum Trot. It wasn't long before major media came knocking on our door—reporters, photographers, and videographers from CBS, NBC, Fox, *Good Morning America, The Oprah Winfrey Show, Reader's Digest, People, Family Circle, Southern Living,* and more.

And all heaven broke loose.

But hell came first.

Eight

Possum Trot Touches America

Jasper, Texas—June 7, 1998. James Byrd Jr., a 49-year-old African American, accepted a ride from three white men—Shawn Berry, Lawrence Brewer, and John King. But instead of taking him home, the men beat Byrd, then chained him by the ankles to the back of their pickup truck.

They got back in the truck and drove, dragging Byrd for about three miles. An autopsy suggested that Byrd was alive for much of the time, until he hit a culvert.

King, Berry, and Brewer dumped the body near a cemetery for blacks, then went off to a barbecue.

King and Brewer were sentenced to death for the crime. Berry got life.

This story hit close to home. That's because my brother-in-law—Donna's brother Kerry—lived in the same apartment building, right next door to the killers!

But it hit home in another way as well. This kind of horror story cast an undeserved shadow over all of East Texas. A few months after the murder, the front page of the *Houston Chronicle* blurted out the headline: "East Texas Racism Subtle but Persistent."

Yes, there were still stubborn pockets of racism. But truth was, for the most part, whites and blacks got along pretty well here in East Texas. And there were also many other good things going on. For instance, there was our story—the story of a little community that had the heart and the guts to adopt 18 of the toughest kids in the foster-care system. And the number was growing.

But those kinds of stories don't make the front pages.

GOOD NEWS FOR A CHANGE

At Child Protective Services, Judy Morgan was thinking like me. Why do stories like this grab all the attention? She called the *Houston Chronicle.* She told them our story.

And what do you know? The same reporter who wrote the article about racism in East Texas was now knocking on our door! He called all of us together for interviews, for pictures. Then he left.

We didn't hear anything for days. Weeks. Months. Other stories seemed to be more important. Our story kept getting pushed back.

Houston, Texas—October 19, 1999. It was over a year now since the racism article ran. At 4 A.M. I got a call. The story of Possum Trot had finally hit the *Houston Chronicle*! I was driving to Houston that morning to catch a plane. As soon as I got to the airport, I picked up the paper. And there it was! "Pining for Homes—Small East Texas Church Becomes Hub for Adoption." Beside the article was a picture of Donna and me, surrounded by families with all these adopted kids. I stood there, staring. It blew my mind. I almost passed out. The miracle of Possum Trot was now being read by thousands of people!

THE "MIRACLE" COMES OUT

About two weeks later, a lady called me from the ABC affiliate in Dallas. They wanted to do a story on us. That same day I got a call from New York. It was Diane Sawyer's office. She wanted to do a story on ABC. She had told the people in Dallas that this was going to be a network story. But then Peter Jennings wanted to do the story. They were going back and forth—who was going to do the story? Diane won. She sent a crew down to Possum Trot.

After that it was like a dam burst. The *Dallas Morning News* picked us up. So did the *San Augustine Tribune. People* magazine did a full article. So did *Reader's Digest, Family Circle,* and *Southern Living.* Our story was aired on National Public Radio's *All Things Considered* and in the United Kingdom on the BBC.

The other major networks called, as well as Fox. And the

story of Possum Trot aired on all of them. We appeared on pro-grams from *Good Morning America* to *48 Hours;* from the Trinity Broadcasting Network to *The 700 Club.*

And then Donna and I found ourselves in a limousine, being driven to the set of *The Oprah Winfrey Show.* It was an amazing time.

All we did was obey God's direction. And God unfolded blessing after blessing. I didn't call any of these people—they called me. And it wasn't because we were in Possum Trot or New York City. It was simply because we were in the will of God. And that's where great things happen.

But it wasn't over.

RENOVATE MY DREAM

In the fall of 2004 my phone rang. It said "Rocket Science" on my caller ID. The lady on the phone explained that Rocket Science was a production company that produced a reality-television show like *Extreme Makeover: Home Edition.* "We want to come down and renovate your home," she said.

The show was called *Renovate My Family (RMF).* I had never heard of it. I wondered if this was a scam. They talked with me for an hour. Talked with Donna for about an hour. We didn't know it, but they were taking us through a process of elimination. And this was to be their last show.

From my point of view, if this was a scam, it was pretty elaborate. They did a psychological profile on me. A drug check. A background check.

And we were chosen. Before we knew it, the lady on the phone was in our home, helping us fill out papers. They were going to totally revamp our house and make it into eight bedrooms.

Something wasn't right. No, by this time I knew it wasn't a scam. But one day this question came out of my mouth before I could think: "What about the children?" The lady paused. I explained. "I've been wanting a facility where these kids can run and play." Maybe I appeared ungrateful. Maybe I was overstepping my bounds. But I had to ask. Besides that, we weren't the only ones who adopted in Possum Trot. Several other adoptive families deserved a blessing like this.

The lady went back to her producers, and they got excited. They scrapped the plans for our house. The producers were now going to build a recreational center for the kids of Possum Trot. And they decided to bless every adoptive family in Possum Trot with brand new furniture for their homes.

Meantime, Johnnie Brown's hospital bill had ballooned to more than twenty thousand. It seemed impossible that she and Fred would ever be able to pay it off.

The *RMF* team asked the hospital for help. And right in front of Johnnie's eyes, they ripped up the bill. The debt was forgiven! All paid for! Johnnie buried her face in her hands and just cried, thanking God.

Now came the part of the show where the producers took the

winning family off to some exotic or fun locale while the family's home was rebuilt. We were all set to go to Hawaii. But because of the new budget for the center, they sent us to Houston.

Sure, it wasn't exactly a tropical paradise. But it was a very nice hotel. The *RMF* producers provided a teacher for the kids to keep up with their school work. And my wife and I just sat around and relaxed—something we didn't get to do very much.

To top things off, the *RMF* team invited a national gospel singer, Kim Burrell, to do a concert with me at a local church in Houston. What a night that was! A night of celebration for what God was doing.

Back home, the crew had fallen in love with the children. They kept saying to themselves, "We're doing this for the kids." But the project soon became one of their toughest challenges.

They built on a parcel of land just outside the neighboring town of Center. The ground was classic East Central Texas red dirt. As the building got underway, the rain came down. And down. And down. The lot turned to classic East Central Texas red mud. Equipment bogged down in the muck. It was a challenge to even walk, as the mud would clutch shoes and yank off boots.

Still, the team worked and worked. Day and night. The place was alive with workers—five hundred of them! They blessed the local economy, buying supplies, packing out the local hotels, getting groceries, and picking up clothes and other things.

Covington Lumber Company in Center donated lumber and

building supplies. "Whatever you need, come and get it," they told the *RMF* crew.

Still, the budget was tight. That's when *RMF* called the Harlem Globetrotters. The famous basketball team came to Center at their own expense to raise funds for the facility! And they left behind 50 official Harlem Globetrotters basketballs for the gymnasium-to-be.

Finally, it was time to bring us back home from Houston. They put us in a van and took us out to the site. The van windows were all blacked out so we couldn't see anything. When we stepped out of the van, we were standing alongside a huge 18-wheeler.

The weather was miserable—cold and gray, with a slow, drizzling rain that chilled us. A bunch of people were huddled behind us. The truck moved. And I went numb. "Lord, what have you done?!"

THE DREAM COMES TRUE

There in front of us was a ten-thousand-square-foot building! Someone handed me a key. "Pastor Martin, here is your key to your brand-new facility!"

I put the key in the doorknob. I turned it. And the door opened to a small heaven. It was a flood of joy, amazement, surprise, and shock. And it was such a contrast to the chilly, gloomy day outside. Here inside, it was bright and warm. And big!

We walked down a short hallway that opened up into a

full-size gymnasium—with a regulation-size basketball court! There was an area set up for music concerts, with an organ and musical instruments for the kids. Giant inflatable crayons were set out for play.

Kids were running. Moms were crying. Dads were praising God. It was one of those moments you never, ever forget.

Diann was there with Nino—our first adopted child in Possum Trot—along with his brother, Randy, and sister, Shanta. The Lathans were there—with all 11 children! Miracle and Milagra and Jamorian, the twins—Shameria and Tameria—Rashaundria, Shenequa, Shereatha, Andre, Justin, and Lovey.

My kids were just as excited as the rest of them. Joshua's eyes were popping! Tyler was there, along with Mercedes, Terri, LaDonna, and Princeton. Fred and Johnnie Brown showed up with little Keiosha and the triplets—Tevin, Terrance, Tiayana.

Outside, there was a row of bikes parked for all the kids. They were smiling and laughing and riding everywhere. Meantime, the triplets took turns politely opening up the gate to the playground for all the other kids to come and play.

The cameras were rolling as *Renovate My Family* asked us what we were going to do with this building. What were our expectations? "We're going to build families," I said. "We're going to build children. We want to educate them, build their self-esteem. As part of that, they're going to work hard."

The interviewer replied, "Pastor Martin, that's okay, but we want these children to laugh and play."

He had me there. When I got the dream for the place, I had heard the laughter as well.

Just off the gym we discovered a full-size, well-equipped, industrial kitchen with top-of-the-line appliances. The pantry was stocked full of food.

We were led to the science room with pictures of planets all around, a full-size photo of the earth on one wall, a powerful telescope in the corner, and all kinds of microscopes and lab equipment. Everything seemed to beg for eager minds to explore.

Next was the playroom, where it felt like we were walking into a storybook forest. There were trees and ponds and birds on the walls, a little play cottage, bright sunflowers and butterflies everywhere, cheery green lily pads for tables, bright red mushrooms for seats, and wooden bookcases packed with stuffed animals and toys. "I felt like a kid!" Donna recalls.

Finally there was the media center with the latest computers, a large-screen TV, educational videos, a set of *Encyclopedia Britannica,* and hundreds of kids' books.

To top it all off, waiting for us outside in the driveway was a brand-new International bus! It was specially painted blue and white with the words "Pineywoods Outreach" on it and "Saving a Generation." Toward the back quarter of the bus was a giant photo of an adult hand reaching out to a child's hand.

To top *that* off, Bebe Wynans showed up at the new center to sing for us! It was a day of blessing after blessing after blessing.

Meantime, the *RMF* team had kept thinking about our

house. They really wanted to help us. They checked back with the office in Los Angeles But it was a no-go. This had already become the biggest *RMF* project ever. The show was over budget.

That's when the *RMF* crew did something truly remarkable. Some of them decided to give up part of their salary from the show. They renovated our entire home out of their own pockets!

The only exception was our bedroom—they had simply run out of money. But everything else was so beautiful, so carefully planned and decorated and furnished. They redid the kids' rooms, gave them all new furniture, and decorated the rooms based on their personalities and interests. And all this at their own expense! For me, the preacher, something unusual happened. This was one of the few times I didn't have anything to say!

Sometime later, it seemed as if all the citizens of Center, Texas, showed up at the Pineywoods Outreach Center. We were all packed together inside the gym, looking up at a giant screen as we watched a special showing of *Renovate My Family* on the Fox network. It was their last episode. The show had folded.

God used the amazing *Renovate My Family* team to bless us "exceeding abundantly above all that we could ask or think." Up to this point, it had seemed like everything was against us. We had believed God, but we didn't see any way through. We just prayed, hoped for a God-sized dream, and did what He told us to do. And that God-sized dream came true.

DONNA REMEMBERS

As Donna walked through the new building, she just shook her head. "God, what did you go and do?" Her mind started thinking back . . .

I kept remembering why God called me to this work. It was all about giving back. These kids had been deprived of so much. Taught all the wrong things. They didn't have the chance to just enjoy life, to laugh. They had to worry about things a child should never have to think about: How am I going to eat? Who is going to curse me? Where will I fit in this next home? Who is going to beat me? Who is going to molest me next?

Even with all the wonderful computers and the exciting things to learn here, something in me just wanted to hear these kids laugh and giggle and have fun.

While folks were marveling over the building, I was marveling over the kids and what they could do now. Parents could drop them off in a safe place where they would never be seen as outcasts. A place where they could run and jump and play. A place where we could build them up. A place where we could teach them not to be takers, but givers—to learn how to give back just as God was teaching me to give back.

As I thought back, I was also impressed with the timing of things. Mama died in February 1996. We first got word about adopting Tyler and Mercedes in February 1997. And we first walked into the new Pineywoods Outreach Center in February 2005.

On Sunday, April 17, 2005, we dedicated the facility to God's glory. The mayor of Center, John D. Windham, made a special declaration and presented us with a special plaque from the city, which read:

Whereas, this facility has been attained through God's blessing and favor with whole-hearted efforts of Rev. W. C. Martin and Bennett Chapel Church; and

Whereas, this magnificent structure will cause an unquestioned impact upon, and become a tremendous asset to, area youth and educational development of the entire community.

NOW, THEREFORE, I, JOHN D. WINDHAM, MAYOR OF THE CITY OF CENTER, TEXAS, and speaking on behalf of the entire City Council and all residents of the community, do hereby extend sincere congratulations and best wishes to all who have worked so faithfully to make this dream become a reality; and I hereby proclaim April 17, 2005, as "Pineywoods Outreach Center Day."

The following year, on March 22, 2006, Shelby County judge Floyd A. Watson signed and sealed a proclamation from Shelby County, which recognized us for "the outstanding contribution made to East Texas, especially Shelby County, in the overall growth and spiritual development of its citizens:

WHEREAS, Pastor WC & Donna Martin have earned the admiration and respect of their community with their dedication to other improvements in the community, especially in the creation of Pineywoods Outreach Ministries . . .

BE IT RESOLVED that this proclamation is prepared for Pastor WC and Donna Martin as an expression of Shelby County's highest appreciation and regard of their distinguished performance as community leaders, and has set an example for others to follow.

For all the negativity we encountered, for all the doubts that were cast our way, we now had more than enough blessings. Yes, it was wonderful to get national media attention for these kids and the parents who adopted them.

But now, we were accepted at home as well. And it was a good feeling.

Since Mama died, we've adopted a total of 72 children. And that's the best feeling of all.

Nine

How?

Many people ask, how did we do it? How did we take on the challenge of adopting some of the toughest kids from the foster-care system?

As you look back over the stories I've shared, you'll see some patterns, patterns that come to light as you travel through Possum Trot.

GRACE

Sometimes as I'm walking through the piney woods of Possum Trot, the sun's rays come through the trees and create pools of light on the dirt path under my feet.

Here's a picture of God's grace. It lights up your day and shows you where to step. Even on the cloudy days or in the midst of a storm, you may not see it, but God's grace is still there. Keep looking up, and sooner or later, you'll find His grace shining through.

Grace is not some nebulous, religious term. It's a practical, everyday reality—a gift of God's undeserved favor toward us. He gives us grace to shine through to these kids, to help them—and us—over the rough spots. Remember, it's God's heart to reach out to these kids. And He gives all the grace to do it well.

God's grace helped Donna when she was dealing with Tyler, who was traumatized by hot-water baths. Grace helped her keep calm for Tyler, calm enough to hear God's voice giving her the strategy: Perfect love drives out all fear.

See, when you do what God has called you to do, He'll give you the tools, the knowledge, and the perseverance to do it. That, my friend, is the light of grace.

UNCONDITIONAL LOVE

On the left is the pathway back to the old Cartwright home-stead—the place we first visited. This little four-room clapboard cottage is overgrown now with weeds and underbrush, but it's alive with memories. This is where Mama Cartwright and her husband, L. J., raised 18 kids, including my wife.

Here is a picture of unconditional love. Mama Cartwright never screamed at her kids, never talked down to them. And she always welcomed the down-and-outers. She taught them all by her example and her courage: "If anything will take you through, love will."

We might not have a lot, but we've got plenty of love—

unconditional love—for all these Possum Trot kids. No matter what these kids do (and they did plenty when they first came here!), we love them through it.

Mommies and daddies had left them. Foster parents had neglected them. They needed to know that someone, somewhere, was finally going to stick with them. Someone, somewhere, was finally going to love them. They tested our love to see if it was the genuine stuff—not a fluffy, sentimental feeling. And they discovered this was the real deal. We really, truly loved them as our own.

When Mercedes lied to me, she needed to know that though I disapproved of her actions, I wasn't going to leave her. I still loved her. My love for Mercedes is not based on how she acts. It's based on who she is—and she's my daughter.

FAITH

Driving through the cool, dark shadows of the woods, you see a rise in the road ahead. As you crest the hill, there's a clearing, and the sun shines on Bennett Chapel, the tan and brown-trim structure on your right with a cross on top. Inside is a beautiful, brightly lit sanctuary where blue-robed choir members sway back and forth with the congregation, singing praises to our God, while our daughter LaDonna brings the Hammond organ to life with rich gospel chords, powered by a Leslie speaker.

It's a place where we sing and shout and worship and enjoy God. It's a place where we "Amen!" as the glory of His Word comes forth to challenge us and to change us. At Bennett Chapel, when the Sunday celebration ends, we don't say that our services have concluded. That's much too restrained. No, instead, at Bennett Chapel, we've "done had church." (And to really say it right, you leave off the *r* in "church.")

Bennett Chapel is a picture of faith. Near this site not long ago was our old wooden church building. I was preaching Murtha's funeral in that little chapel, crammed to the brim with congregants, when we heard this loud *Pop!* The floor had collapsed! A whole row of people politely stood up from their pews and moved back. The floor had completely separated from the wall and caved in. The roof started to sag.

We had maybe 50 active members in the church and about three hundred dollars in the building-fund treasury. Without enough money or manpower, it looked impossible to build a new sanctuary. I talked to the Lord about it, and He gave me faith to believe. I put an article in the paper. And God sent people in from everywhere to help us. United Builders came and volunteered 52 manpower weeks of time to help us. Promise Keepers and the Southern Baptist Association pitched in. Workers donated their labor. We got building supplies at half price. Normally, a church like this would run seven to eight hundred thousand dollars. We got this beautiful building for a hundred and fifty thousand.

God helped me see it before it came to be—His gift of faith to me.

When Theresa and Glen Lathan were faced with adopting

three more kids for a total of 11 children, they shook their heads. "We can't do it!" It looked impossible. But God gave them the gift of faith when He whispered in their hearts and said, *Yes, you can!*

Now they have a legacy—a legacy of kids who have been rescued. Kids who have been redeemed. Kids who have hopes and futures where there were none. God's gift of faith helped them to see beyond where they were and grab hold of the impossible. As a result, the lives of several children have been changed forever.

COMMUNITY AS FAMILY

Next door to Bennett Chapel is another sanctuary, a sanctuary of loved ones dead and gone, their tombstones dating back to the 1800s. Donna's parents—Mama and L. J.—are buried here on part of the Cartwright portion of the cemetery. You'll find three prominent family names here. Along with the Cartwrights are the Swindles and the McCowins—all of us tracing back our roots five or six generations to the freed slaves who started this community.

Here is a picture of how our community relates as family. We're really one big family here—through the thick and thin of life, right up till death itself. If a family is having trouble with a child and needs some help, they don't call Child Protective Services. They call on a neighbor or a nearby relative. Sometimes, that child may stay with someone else for a while till things get straightened out. It's how we relate as family. We're in this together.

When Diann was too overloaded to handle three boys, instead of sending one or two children back to the foster system, Donna and I took one of them in as our own. When Theresa Lathan's sister and brother-in-law died, she and her husband took in three more children.

And if a child is in somebody else's home and happens to act up, that child is in as much trouble as if he were in his own home. We look out for one another here in Possum Trot—and that includes the children.

ACCEPTANCE

The intersection of Farm Roads 3471S and 2545 is where the two main roads of Possum Trot intersect. We call this The Crossroads. If there were a traffic light in Possum Trot, this is probably where it would be.

On a typical summer night in Possum Trot, you'll hear the crickets singing under the stars. And you'll hear the laughter of kids. This is where the kids gather to tell jokes and stories and visit with one another.

The Crossroads is a picture of acceptance. You won't find any distinction between the adopted kids and the biological kids. The kids don't say, "She's my adopted sister" or "He's my biological brother." They say, "She's my sister" or "He's my brother."

Seven-year-old Miracle Lathan had to learn acceptance the hard way. Remember how it seemed like an invasion when five sisters came in and stole away her mom and dad? She called them "those girls" with disdain. But even at age seven, Miracle Lathan learned to reach out of herself, to go beyond her own selfishness. She started, gradually, to share her toys and dolls. And it wasn't too long before she no longer referred to them as "those girls." Instead, they became "my sisters." She had learned to accept them. They were family.

COMMITMENT

Take a moment and just breathe in all the beauty around you. It's something, isn't it? We're at the edge of the Sabine National Forest—a lush woodland of towering pine trees, namesake of the piney woods.

The tall trees give a picture of a deep-rooted commitment over the long haul. That commitment inspired all of Mama Cartwright's 18 children to stay here in Possum Trot, because they were committed to one another and this community.

Johnnie Brown endured asthma, fibromyalgia, diabetes, and high blood pressure and even death itself in her commitment to take care of her newly adopted triplets and their little sister. The kids would follow her around the house. These little ones had been abandoned by adults they had trusted and were terrified that Johnnie would leave them. She wasn't about to let them down. She endured with a rock-solid commitment.

"Sure they have problems," she says, "but to look at where

they've come from and where they are now, it's just amazing. They're very well-mannered children." And she loves their company. "We talk a lot. Play games together. And they tell me how much they love me. Lots of hugging!"

Johnnie Brown's commitment saved the lives and futures of four children. But what if she hadn't acted? Where would these kids be today? That's a small picture of what's at stake for our entire nation. It's no exaggeration to say that the future of an entire generation of abandoned kids hangs in the balance.

Ten

Your Turn for a Miracle

Think about it.

Moses was adopted. So was Esther. And Samuel. God does miraculous things—powerful things—through adopted kids.

There's something about children that is close to God's heart. When busy disciples brushed the little children aside to make way for the adults, Jesus rebuked them. And He called the children to come close. "Do not hinder them," He said, "for the kingdom of heaven belongs to such as these" (Matthew 19:14).

And among children, God holds a special place for the orphans. If you ever want to rile up God (please note this would be pretty stupid), just try messing with one of these little ones. "Do not take advantage of a widow or an orphan," He warns us. "If you do and they cry out to me, I will certainly hear their cry" (Exodus 22:22, 23). And then you're in Really Big Trouble. God is fierce, and He will personally defend the fatherless (see Deuteronomy 10:18), hurling curses on all who treat them unjustly (see Deuteronomy 27:19).

Then again, if you ever want to win God's favor, take care of a child who's been abandoned by Mom and Dad. James calls this true religion—the real thing. "Religion that God our Father accepts as pure and faultless is this: to look after orphans and widows in their distress and to keep oneself from being polluted by the world" (James 1:27).

Think about this—when you reach out to the orphan, you're reaching out to one of your own. Because we're *all* adopted. God "predestined us to be adopted as his sons through Jesus Christ" (Ephesians 1:5). God rescued us from bondage, from fear, and He adopted us as His sons and daughters. He gave us His name and gave us a new start. So now we can call Him Daddy (*Abba,* as in Romans 8:15).

This Awesome Dad has given us a rich gift, and He wants us to pass it on. He longs to reach out to the kids who have been left behind, to the kids who are hopelessly shifted from foster home to foster home. And He wants to use our arms, your arms.

God calls us to rescue these kids from bondage and fear, and adopt them as our sons and daughters. To give each one a new name and a new start.

Through us, God worked a miracle here in Possum Trot. Is it your turn for a miracle?

"But we already have a good-size family."

Remember Glen and Theresa Lathan? They already had three kids when they decided to adopt five sisters. And then, when Theresa's sister and brother-in-law died, they adopted three more, for a total of 11 kids. They discovered great rewards, including the reward of knowing they did the right thing. And the reward of love coming back to them—elevenfold!

"We don't have enough money to take care of any more kids."

Possum Trot is in Shelby County, one of the poorest counties in Texas, with an average annual income under thirty thousand dollars. Our bottom line: We took in the kids, and God provided.

"I'm only a single mom."

Think about Diann Sparks, the single working mom who decided to take in not one, but two boys. It was a stretch for her, but now these boys are such a powerful blessing to Diann, it would tear her up if they ever had to go back into the system. She's determined that they won't. She loves them too much.

"We're already empty nesters."

Calvin and Jewel Williams had two daughters in their 20s who were just about ready to move on from home. The free lifestyle of the empty-nest years was right within reach. But they felt this call from God to adopt. So they started parenting all over again with a little five-year-old boy named Kendric.

Kendric is now so much a part of the family that he even physically *looks* like he's part of the family. And Calvin and Jewel have discovered the joy of a son. Kendric has been a true blessing to them and has enriched their lives in many ways. Their dream for him is to go to college, get a good job, and take care of a wife and family of his own. "And maybe reach back and help his old mom and dad," adds Jewel with a smile.

"I'm too old."

Johnnie and Fred Brown were grandparents, with kids in their 20s and 30s, when they decided to adopt a set of triplets and their little sister.

They knew God called them to do it. It was extremely tough on Johnnie, but they both sowed diligently and sowed well. And now they have some of the most well-mannered, adorable children in Possum Trot. Mom and Dad draw from their love. And they also draw from the knowledge that they've rescued some precious kids from abandonment and a lifetime of pain.

"We've got special circumstances."

You'll remember our son Princeton was permanently brain-damaged—a significant challenge in itself—but we decided to adopt more kids anyway. (When God says do something, we just do it and He helps us work out the details.)

Princeton was mostly off to himself. He would spend a lot of time in his room, playing his guitar or listening to gospel music. We sat down with our new kids and told them that Princeton was a special boy who needed special attention. He also needed their love.

And these kids got it. As they reached out to Princeton, they got their eyes off their own troubles. God birthed something in them— a heartfelt care for someone who was worse off than they were.

It was hard for people to understand Princeton's slurred and garbled speech, but Terri discovered Princeton's "language" and learned to interpret what he was saying. Mercedes often volunteered to help him clean his room and would help him lay out his clothes for church. At night the kids would remind him to get his shower, and when Princeton wanted to hear the Bible, the kids would read to him.

Something precious happened that we couldn't have foreseen. Princeton opened up and came out of his little world. He learned how to communicate better, how to think of others first, and how to share—*and our kids taught him!*

"It's really not convenient."

To be blunt, this isn't about you. It's about the children. It's not convenient for a two-year-old girl to waddle around in the same diaper all day, alone in her house. It's not convenient for a six-year-old to steal from the store so he can feed his little sister at home. It's not convenient for a five-year-old boy to be beaten up by a drunken dad.

No, I'm not sensationalizing. These are real-life stories happening right around you—in your town. You don't foster and adopt for your own gratification. You do it for the kids' sake. You do it with the same unconditional love Jesus gives you.

I've been as frank and honest as I can, giving you some of the roughest cases we've had with adoption. Yeah, it's tough. Adopting isn't for wimps. But when you partner with God to rescue a child, when God chooses you to pluck her out of a living death, there is no reward like it—to hear her laugh for the first time, to see her chase her newfound friends in the playground, to feel her little arms around you as you kiss her cheek good night.

And now I'm going to give an unusual challenge from an author.

Stop reading.

Take five minutes—right now—to pray and see what God is saying to you about adoption. Are *you* supposed to adopt? If so, what's the next practical step He's telling you to take? If you're not supposed to adopt, what is God saying about supporting families who do adopt?

Okay, stop reading now. I'll wait right here while you pray . . .

LISTENING TO GOD

You may need to set aside some more time to know God's heart for your situation. Do. If God says *Yes*, or if you're not sure, there are some practical steps you can take right now.

You can either adopt through a state agency or a private adoption agency. For a state agency, check with your state's department of social services. This is usually a cost-free or low-cost option. Private adoption agencies offer another alternative. Refer to the appendix on page 133 for more information.

Keep in mind, God challenged Possum Trot to take the hard cases—the older children. And the stories I've told you are some of the most challenging. I didn't want to sugarcoat the process. But I don't want to shortchange the reality of the tremendous rewards either. There is no feeling like seeing how God's love—coming through you—can transform a child. And change his or her future forever.

But maybe God's calling on you is a little different. Maybe He's calling you to adopt a forgotten baby. Either way, you're rescuing a child. Either way, you're caring for the fatherless.

Eleven

Bring the Miracle Home

There's a danger in reading a book like this. You might get the impression that Possum Trot is a unique community, uniquely suited to adopting kids. And what works in Possum Trot wouldn't work elsewhere.

You'd be wrong, because most Christians *have* a community just like Possum Trot—a community that welcomes kids with grace, unconditional love, faith, a sense of family, acceptance, and commitment.

It's called the church.

If the church is all God has called it to be, then it's the ideal refuge for the forgotten children of America. A place where adoptive families can find the support and the community they need to raise these children well. See, the miracle of Possum Trot isn't just for us. It's a miracle that can be—and should be—duplicated in churches all across this nation.

If our little church of two hundred members can adopt 72 kids, how many can *your* church take in?

If the church is championing the case against abortion, then we'd best be ready to "play catch" when waves of unwanted children inundate the system.

After all, every child deserves unconditional love. Not one child should be left abandoned. It's our call as the church to reach out to these little ones with the love and good news of Jesus.

Jesus Himself said, "Let the little children come to me, and do not hinder them, for the kingdom of God belongs to such as these" (Matthew 19:14). The goal is to see children come to Christ. And what better place for that to happen than in loving, adoptive families? Jesus took the children in His arms, put His hands on them, and blessed them. Are we ready now to do the same?

Yes, there are challenges to adoption. The world says an adopted child will always feel loneliness and rejection. The world says there can never be a strong bonding with the adoptive parent. That's what the *world* says. Here's what the Word says:

"With man this is impossible, but with God all things are possible." (Matthew 19:26)

I can do all things through Christ who strengthens me. (Philippians 4:13, NKJV)

Christ is the key. And with His power, with His wisdom, you will gain His victory for your child and you. I'm not just saying words. I'm saying the *Word,* which I have seen in action.

For any challenge you face with adoption, all the answers you need can be found in a best-selling book that I strongly recommend to you. Get it. Read it. Do it. I don't recommend books often, or this strongly, but here is my unabashed plug for this one. It's called "The Bible." (Hey, now what do you expect from a preacher?)

Seriously, God's Word has everything you need to know for life, including adoption. Take time to dig in. Get into the Word, and let the Word get into you. "Then you will know the truth, and the truth will set you free" (John 8:32).

As a parent, start here with Ephesians 1:4-6:

> He chose us in him before the creation of the world to be
> holy and blameless in his sight. In love he predestined us to
> be adopted as his sons through Jesus Christ, in accordance
> with his pleasure and will—to the praise of his glorious
> grace, which he has freely given us in the One he loves.

Here's the model: God chose us. He expects the best from us. He loves us and adopts us. Through Jesus, He freely gives us His grace.

We chose our child. We expect the best from her. We love her and adopt her. Through Jesus, we freely give her grace.

God rescued us from darkness and bondage and brought us

into the light and freedom. We rescue our child from darkness and bondage and bring her into the light and freedom.

As you pray, God will show you the way through, because when you adopt, you're doing something that's close to His heart. After all, God Himself is a Father to the fatherless. Ask God for His input to train up your child in His ways.

Beware that as you rescue your child physically, you will need to also rescue your child spiritually. The enemy has come to steal, kill, and destroy him. Your job is to defend your child and pray protection over him daily.

Your obedience to God is a vital part of His protection as well (see Exodus 34:6, 7).

Pray for the full armor of God (see Ephesians 6:10-18) to cover him and your family. Pray for the covering of the blood of Jesus for all of you—the blood that helps you overcome the enemy (see Revelation 12:11).

Then, go to war for your child. Use the sword of the Spirit—which is the Word of God—against the enemy. Pray verses like these:

"I have given you authority to trample on snakes and scorpions and to overcome all the power of the enemy; nothing will harm you." (Luke 10:19)

"I will give you the keys of the kingdom of heaven; whatever you bind on earth will be bound in heaven, and

whatever you loose on earth will be loosed in heaven."
(Matthew 16:19)

For we do not wrestle against flesh and blood, but against
principalities, against powers, against the rulers of the darkness of this age, against spiritual hosts of wickedness in the
heavenly places. Therefore take up the whole armor of God,
that you may be able to withstand in the evil day, and having done all, to stand. (Ephesians 6:10-13, NKJV)

You are in a battle for the soul of your child. The Enemy
wants your child back. But take courage. This is a winnable battle
because it's a war that Jesus has already won. Through His victory, you are more than a conqueror (Romans 8:37).

Now, as God leads you, go after the specific areas of concern.
Here are some ways the Enemy commonly attacks in cases of
abuse: rejection, abandonment, fear, insecurity, lying, anger and
rage, violence, rebellion, addictions (including alcohol and drugs),
poverty, slavery, wandering, idolatry, and sexual immorality (including perversion, seduction, adultery, fornication).

Pray with the Holy Spirit as your guide and God's Word as
your weapon. For instance, when coming against fear, speak the
promise of Scripture over your child:

There is no fear in love. But perfect love drives out fear.
(1 John 4:18)

God has not given us a spirit of fear, but of power and of
love and of a sound mind. (2 Timothy 1:7, NKJV)

Here's an example of using Scripture as part of your prayer:

Father God, I thank You that Your perfect love casts out fear
from my daughter. I pray Your perfect love will fill her now
and cast out all fear, in Jesus' name. I declare over my daughter that God has not given her a spirit of fear. I proclaim that
God has given her a spirit of power, of love, and of a sound
mind.

Make sure you pray the counterpart blessing—in this case,
love. (This is the fun part!) Here, we can use 1 Corinthians 13—
the love chapter—as our prayer:

Father God, defend my daughter. May others be patient with
her, and kind to her, never envious of her. Let her never be
boastful or proud. Guard her from rudeness, from those who
are selfish. Protect her from anger, from those who would
keep a record of wrongs against her, from those who delight
in evil. Fill her with the joy of Your truth. As she learns to
trust in Your protection, restore her hope, and give her the
strength of perseverance. May she come to know Your truth
deep inside—that Your love for her will never fail.

The ultimate redemption is when God's love transforms your daughter, and she becomes a model of love for others:

> Father God, as Your love becomes part of my daughter's life, I pray she will be a model of love to others. May she be patient and kind, never envious, boastful, or proud. I pray she will refrain from rudeness, from self-seeking. I pray she will not be easily angered and will keep no record of wrongs. May she never delight in evil, but rejoice with the truth, always protecting, always trusting, always hoping, always persevering. As Your love never fails her, may her love never fail others.

DISCIPLINE IS LOVE

A few other things to remember . . .

Don't be afraid to correct your child. It's a sign of your love.

"The LORD disciplines those he loves, as a father the son he delights in" (Proverbs 3:12).

Your child needs boundaries. It's part of your love and protection for him. Note that because of prior abuse, corporal punishment may not be advised. There are more ways to correct, such as time-outs, taking away privileges, and so on.

Remember, you are the example of a godly walk to your children. They're watching you!
So many adults have let your children down. It's time to be the adult they can trust, the adult they can follow.

Meditate on Psalm 68 and see what God shows you about your adopted child.

> Sing to God, sing praise to his name,
> > extol him who rides on the clouds—
> > his name is the LORD—
> > and rejoice before him.
> A father to the fatherless, a defender of widows,
> > is God in his holy dwelling.
> God sets the lonely in families,
> > he leads forth the prisoners with singing. (verses 4-6)

And now, it's time to take our last tour of Possum Trot.

Twelve

The Beginning of the Road

We're heading back now, down Farm Road 2625. This land all around us used to be farms—fields full of sorghum, cotton, peanuts, peas, or ribbon cane. There are just a few farms left now, like the one up here on the left, where Bishop Zephaniah Swindle lives. Bishop is Donna's godfather. He's been a preacher for over 50 years. But he's got another congregation—his pride and joy. It's a herd of his own cows. Roll down your window and you can hear him calling to his cattle.

Not many of his kind left nowadays. Most folks in Possum Trot work at one of the chicken-processing plants over in Center or at the hardwood-floor plant.

A hard left on 2545 . . . on your right, under the shade of that grove of trees, is where folks gather to play dominos over an old wooden table. A couple of doors down, you'll find the little yellow house of 98-year-old Jane Ann Land, the oldest resident of Possum Trot.

It was about 10 years ago now that the miracle started. Ten years since Diann took in the very first adopted child in Possum Trot—Nino. Today, there are 72 adopted children.

Now, as we leave Possum Trot, it's a good time to bring you up to date on the ones I told you about.

WHERE ARE THESE KIDS NOW?

Diann's kids . . .
Nino, 13

I can tell you where Nino is right now—he's up ahead there, riding a horse. Hard to believe how much that boy has grown. He was four years old then. He's now 13. From the get-go, Nino fit right into the family, and right into school. As if he'd been here a long time.

Nino is the outdoor kid. Loves to play baseball and football. Loves to fish and go hunting with his uncle. And he loves to ride horses. His dream is to one day go to Louisiana State University.

Randy, 11

Nino's brother Randy was five years old and required a lot of attention. But he took to Diann and quickly became her "prayer baby." On days when she was feeling down and out after a long day at work, Randy would tell her, "Mama you don't have to cook. Just take your bath and lie down." And he'd go fix some scrambled eggs for her to eat and pray over her. "Father, take care of my mama. She doesn't feel good today."

To this day, he's a very encouraging kid. "Mama, it's okay," he'll say when they face a challenge. "We'll just pray about this. God's gonna fix it. He'll work it out."

He's 11 now. He wants to go to college, but not too far away, because he wants to take care of his mom. His goal is to be a police officer, because he wants to help people.

Catching up with our own kids . . .
Tyler, 11

Tyler started out very shy. He had trouble fitting in. Made bad grades. Now he's making good grades in school and really likes math. His dream? He wants to be a mechanic, or a policeman.

Donna gets a kick out of how Tyler teases her when he wants her to buy something for him or get a pizza or go to a movie. "Mom, you know I'm your son. You know I'm your baby. You've got to do that for me. I don't know about the rest, but you know I'm your son."

Mercedes, 14

When Mercedes first came to us, she was making bad grades. Now she's making As and Bs. Mercedes is determined to be a doctor, specifically, an anesthesiologist.

Donna describes Mercedes as a classy personality—she loves to dress up in long dresses and skirts and heels. She also loves to please her mother and cares very much how Mom feels about her. "Mom, how do I look in this?" "Mom, can you clip my hair?" "How does my hair look? Should I wear it down or wear it up?" Donna calls her "my outgoing glamour girl."

Terri, 17

God rescued Terri from a very ugly world and has been healing the bitterness in her. She now has hope and sees life as something beautiful. She has developed a real talent for doing hair and wants to be a cosmetologist.

Terri enjoys going to school, where she's on the honor roll, with an A average. She is a very caring person. And no matter if she falls in life, she gets up again. "Terri is like grace to me," Donna says. "New every day."

"I used to hang out in the street and do ungodly things such as drugs," says Terri. "The people I lived with didn't go to church and didn't want me to be part of a church. Now I understand I need to go to church to become the person I need to be." Terri enjoys singing in the choir at Bennett Chapel and loves leading the praise dance team at church—a group of 15 called the BC Rejoicers.

Terri believes God is leading her to go to college in Beaumont. In addition to cosmetology, she's also thinking about becoming a nurse, going into business, or becoming a counselor to help abused children. "I know what they go through," she says. "I can help them."

Joshua, 13

When Joshua was small, he was literally locked away in a room with no light. When he came to us, the little boy was in a world all to himself. He had trouble focusing, and he struggled with bad grades. But we believed in him, and we told him we weren't going to accept any less than his best.

Joshua's smart. He just had to apply himself. We stayed on him, and he worked up to a really good year at school, where he has developed a love of learning and especially enjoys reading, math, and science.

Joshua joined the school football team, plays the trumpet, loves to draw, and enjoys the outdoors. He can tell you which tree this is and what insect that is.

This last year was tough on him—he fell behind a bit in school, so we took him out of football. But he knows we're not going to give up on him. And Josh himself is an overcomer.

"He's my smiling boy," says Donna. "Just give him those

encouraging words and he'll feed off it." Even his eyes smile. He always says, "When I grow up, I want to become a preacher, like my daddy." And those eyes will light up, with a big smile on his face.

Calvin and Jewel Williams's son, Kendric, 13

Kendric started off shy, but that didn't last long. He's very social now and enjoys getting out with other people. You'll often see Kendric walking up and down the dirt roads of Possum Trot with his friends or playing basketball.

Calvin and Jewel say Kendric loves to play games on Xbox and PlayStation, but he's also very helpful around the house.

From the time he was little, Kendric was honest about his mistakes. "If he got into trouble, he'd come and tell you," says Dad. "He wouldn't hold back."

Dad also notes that once Kendric sets his mind on a goal, he goes for it and gives it everything he's got. Kendric's dream is to play professional basketball or football. But if that doesn't work out, he's talked about becoming a doctor.

Glen and Theresa Lathan's kids . . . Shameria, 12

When she was first here, she was off balance emotionally. She had trouble keeping still. Now Shameria has grown up into a tall young girl with dreams of becoming a professional basketball player. She's working hard, preparing herself to play on the seventh-grade team.

Glen says she's definitely a leader and gets along well with other people. Theresa appreciates how kind Shameria is to others. She loves to help people, especially the older folks. She'll go over to an elderly person's house to wash her dishes, take out the trash, and sweep the floor. At church she'll take note when older people walk in—she'll walk over and offer to carry their bags and Bibles for them.

Tameria, 12

Shameria's twin sister used to be extremely quiet, hardly saying anything. She was very afraid.

"We all loved her, no matter what," says Glen. "We let her know she didn't have to worry anymore about where she was going to sleep. She had a permanent home here." That constant reassurance seemed to help.

Theresa says when Tameria first came, even the smallest things would frighten her, like a fly in the air or anything that moved quickly. She was afraid that if she went outside, a bug would get on her. "We couldn't even get her to go outside to play."

One day, as her brothers and sisters were out in the yard playing, she ventured out to the doorstep, but no farther. The next day, she stood in the same spot, and they called to her. "Come on out, we're here!" Slowly, she started inching her way down. Eventually, in a day or so, she joined them in the yard.

Tameria has outgrown her fears, and now she converses well with others. Her dream is to be a doctor. And she has another dream. She wants to do just like her mama and daddy, and adopt children.

Rashaundria, 13

Rashaundria wants to be a lawyer. She used to be very clingy and very afraid her mama would abandon her. When she got off the bus from school, she'd run home as quick as she could, open the door, and holler out "Mama!" She wanted to make sure her mother hadn't left her.

Rashaundria's grades used to be really low. But her parents kept working with her. Now she makes nothing but As and Bs.

Shenequa, 14

Shenequa was very outspoken when she first came. (She still is!) At only six years old, Shenequa felt the responsibility to take care of her sisters. And it was hard to break her of that. She considered herself the mother for the twins.

When the other girls were folding clothes or cleaning, she'd tell them what to do and how to do it. If Theresa corrected one of them, Shenequa would find out why and tell them, "You don't have to do that." If Mom told them to straighten their room, Shenequa would say, "Don't worry, I'll do that for you."

Mom and Dad had to constantly remind Shenequa that she didn't have to be the mother anymore. She's outgrown that now. And her dream is to be a nurse. She wants to take care of people.

Shenequa has come a long way. She was so far behind in school—making Ds and Fs—that she had to take special classes. Now she's in high school, taking regular classes, including algebra, and doing a good job.

Shereatha, 16

When Shereatha first came, she was extremely nervous. At times, she would just freeze up with fear. She depended on someone else to do everything for her. As Theresa puts it, "She was afraid to trust herself."

When it came time to learn how to drive, Shereatha was sure of one thing. "I don't think I can do that!" Mom and Dad had a hard time teaching her, but they didn't give up.

One evening, when Dad finally got her to drive, she turned off the main road to go to their house and ran the car into some bushes. She was a mess. But Dad kept reassuring her. "That's all right. We all make mistakes." He didn't get upset with her and tried to be as calm and steady as possible for her. Mom and Dad both encouraged her that learning to drive was part of her growing up. As they worked with her, she got better and better.

Now, Shereatha drives all by herself—no problem. She loves to play basketball and was chosen All-District Player of the Year. She also runs track and almost went to state—during her very first year on the team. As Shereatha says, "I'm *fast!*"

Shereatha's dream? To be an occupational therapist, working with small children.

❧

Andre, 15

Andre's the sports guy—he plays basketball and football. But when he first arrived in Possum Trot, he was a very angry little boy. He stayed that way a long time. If somebody said something he disagreed with, or if Theresa and Glen didn't show him the attention he wanted, Andre would storm off to his room. "He'd hit on stuff," Mom says. "He'd kick stuff. Pound on the walls."

Dad says Andre would snap at the other kids in ways that showed he had been abused. "It was like he had something balled up inside him. He had to let it out."

His parents talked to him frequently. Mom would remind him, "None of this that happened to you was your fault." And Dad would tell him, "You don't have to hold stuff inside, Andre. You can talk about it. We're here to listen."

Their talks and prayers worked. When Andre was finally convinced of their love over the long haul, he began to let go of the anger. He is no longer off to himself.

Today, Andre is a happy young man. "He'll sit around with

us when we play cards or dominos together," Dad says. He loves to joke and laughs all the time now.

Andre's dream is to play basketball in college. And there's a good chance he'll do just that.

✥

Justin, 13

Justin was always active, always moving. Even if he was going off to brush his teeth, he'd take off in a run! Justin plays football now, and he's an accomplished running back. It seems all he talks about is football. It's no surprise he has his sights set on becoming a football player.

✥

Lovey, 13

As a little girl, she always kept to herself, playing by herself, talking to her dolls. Lovey has turned around dramatically. She's much more outgoing nowadays, and in fact, she's training to be a cheerleader. Her dream is to become a teacher.

✥

And finally, Fred and Johnnie Brown's kids . . .
Keiosha, 9

Despite the profanity and stubbornness, little Keiosha was actually very shy around people when she first came to the Brown family. But now her confidence has blossomed. She's in school

The Martin family

plays—acting in front of audiences—and her mama says she's very good. In a recent Christmas play, she was Rudolph the Red-Nosed Reindeer.

Keiosha is highly intelligent and loves to read. At a local school-district event, she won an accelerated-readers award in her class.

One day, Keiosha hopes to be an actress.

Tevin, 10

Tevin was always the leader of the group. He still is. Johnnie notes that he's unusually wise for his age. Tevin also writes songs. He'll disappear for 30 minutes in his room, come back, and sing a song he just wrote.

One time, Tevin narrated a Christmas play for his school. As soon as he was finished, he ran down from the stage and gave his mom a big hug. "Mama, did you see what I did?"

"I sure did! You did a wonderful job!"

Tevin has two dreams for the future: to be a music writer/producer. And to become a preacher.

Tiayana, 10

At two-and-a-half years old, Tiayana was extremely withdrawn. She wouldn't play with the other kids. She never smiled. And she had trouble talking. She knew no one would understand her, so she kept silent.

But Johnnie heard her. And understood her. Every day, Johnnie would give Tiayana some exclusive one-on-one time. She'd go to Tiayana's room and play games with her like Connect 4 or Candy Land or Old Maid. She'd read to Tiayana. And when Tiayana was a little older, Johnnie would ask her to read back to her.

Tiayana started coming to her mom and talking with her. "Oh, my baby," Johnnie would say. "Come to me!" Johnnie would encourage her, even if Tiayana was saying just one word. "My baby's talking!" she'd say. Johnnie started by repeating words back to her and communicating with her.

Even now, Tiayana is not very talkative. "But she sure can smile," says her mom. She says Tiayana is a very confident, very mature young lady.

Before Tiayana even started prekindergarten, Johnnie taught her and her siblings how to spell and read. In a reading competition recently, Tiayana took second place in her entire school. Tiayana's goal? "I want to be a teacher."

✤

Terrance, 10

A boiling anger raged inside Terrance. He would fight at a moment's notice, grabbing his brother's neck and slamming him to the floor, or running his brother's head into the wall.

After a lot of prayer and love, Terrance has rounded out to be a very happy kid, and very playful. He's no longer rough. Instead he's athletic, playing football and basketball—and he's good. His dream is to become a professional football player. His mama can't talk him into anything else.

Terrance made the lowest grades. But now, he and his brother and sisters are all on the honor roll at school.

Take a good look. These aren't mishaps or mistakes. These are kids with hopes, dreams, and accomplishments. The very same kids society was going to throw away. Just look at how God has redeemed them!

WE SAID YES TO THE KIDS

The world said no to these kids. But Possum Trot said yes. And the world's a better place for it, with the blessing of 72 kids—each one with a new hope and bright future.

I take their stories with me as I give talks all around the country, encouraging people to remember the forgotten children. Many tell me this was the message they needed to help them make their decision to adopt. In Columbus, Ohio, I spoke up for five little kids in a group home who needed a family to take them in. After my talk, all of them were adopted. It's exciting to see how God is using our story—the miracle of Possum Trot—to bring more kids home.

I often think back to that afternoon when Donna stood on the back porch and God whispered in her heart, *Give back. Foster and adopt.* That afternoon changed our lives. Changed our congregation. Changed our town. It's my dream that one day that afternoon will change a nation . . .

And now, my friend, I bring you back to where our journey started, on Farm Road 3471. At the end of the pavement.

And the end of this book.

But turn around, and you'll see a new perspective. After all, this may very well be the beginning of a new road for you.

A Call to My Fellow Pastors

As we think about these stories, we might ask ourselves, *How can a human being do these awful things to a child?* But here's a question closer to home: *How can we close our eyes to a child like this?*

So, where is the church? God commanded us to look after the fatherless. Why don't we obey?

There's been more than enough talk. Since 1987, the number of children in foster care has nearly doubled. It's time to do something. If we don't, we're about to lose a generation of kids. I challenge you to join with me in saying, "Not on our watch!"

Father God called on His Son, Jesus, to give up glory and royalty—His "comfort zone"—to come down to a dark world to rescue us, to share His glory, to adopt us into His royal family. And now He's calling on us to step out of our world of convenience to rescue these kids. To save a generation.

He gave up His life to save us. Can we give up our comfort? No longer can we afford to sit around idly, waiting for state agencies or Congress or the president to solve the problem of 134,000 children who need adopting. This is *our* responsibility as a church.

It's time to stop talking about how bad these children are, and start reaching them with the transforming love of Jesus. The Devil loves to steal, kill, and destroy—and he especially enjoys stealing, killing, and destroying children. They're defenseless. Easy marks if they don't have a mom or dad to pray protection over them.

He has bound thousands of children into a dark world of chaos, where adults slap them, sexually abuse them, and leave them abandoned, locked up in houses without even food to eat.

The church has an anointing, a power, and a mandate to make a difference in the world. It's our job to free these kids from captivity.

It's time for the church to stand up. To come out of its addiction to comfort. I challenge the church to take up the cause of these children. God has already done His part. It's our turn now.

It's time for the Enemy to realize that he's not going to win. It's time for the Enemy to tremble. It's time for the gates of hell around these children to fall. It's time for the church to prevail. It's time to rescue these children out of darkness and bondage and bring them into the light.

It's time to bring them home.

—Pastor W. C. Martin

Note: Check with local government adoption agencies. They'll be glad to come to talk to your church or church group at no charge, just as Child Protective Services came to Bennett Chapel. Look up your local department of social services, human services, or child welfare agency.

Appendix:

Help for Those Considering Adoption

THE NUMBERS AND THE HOPE

There are approximately 134,000 children in the United States without a home.[1] These are kids who have been neglected, abandoned, and abused. Now they're languishing in a foster-care system, moving from house to house to house.

Nearly 82 million American adults have considered adopting a child. All it would take is one adult out of roughly every 500 people in that group to adopt, so that *all 134,000 children would be able to "come home" to a permanent family.*

AN OVERVIEW

There isn't a national standard for adopting children. It's different from state to state. A few things to know:

- You don't have to own your own home or have a certain salary to adopt.

---

1. All facts and statistics in this section are from the 2002 National Adoption Attitudes Survey, sponsored by the Dave Thomas Foundation for Adoption and the Evan B. Donaldson Adoption Institute.

• You don't have to be the same race as your adopted child.

• Agencies are looking for parents who will provide a safe, stable, and loving environment for the child.

• You can adopt through a public agency, a private agency, or arrange an "independent" adoption, using an intermediary, such as an attorney or physician. (Make sure you're confident in their ethics and their expertise in adoption laws—ask for references.)

15 Steps to Adopt Your Child

1. Gather information.

If you're thinking about adoption, be aware that adoption can sometimes take awhile. It's somewhat like going through an obstacle course. But in the end, giving a child a home and raising him in a family that loves him can be one of the most fulfilling rewards you'll ever experience.

To get started, log on to www.family.org and type "adoption" in the search box for a list of excellent resources from Focus on the Family. Or contact the organization below:

Voice of the Orphan

Family Life

P.O. Box 7111

Little Rock, Arkansas 72223

Within the United States, call 1-800-FL-TODAY
(1-800-358-6329) 24 hours a day, or 1-877-FL-TODAY.
Outside the United States, call 501-223-8663.
www.voiceoftheorphan.org

2. Think it over. Pray it over.

Remember these kids don't need perfect parents, just committed parents—committed to love them, encourage them, and guide them. Some important qualities you'll need include:
- A love of children and parenting
- Patience and perseverance
- A good sense of humor
- The ability to love unconditionally

Some questions to ask yourself:
- Why am I adopting?
- Do my spouse and I work well as a team? Are we both committed to adopting?
- Does our lifestyle give us the time and resources we'll need to raise our child? (Note that financial assistance is available.)

3. Choose which kind of adoption.

Do you hope to adopt a newborn, or are you going to adopt a child from the foster-care system? Are you going to adopt within the United States, or will your child come from another country?

4. Check out financial assistance.

There is an amazing number of resources you can tap into for help with the finances of adopting. Although the cost varies depending on which kind of adoption you want, keep in mind that in many cases you can adopt a child at no cost.

If there is a cost, your employer may offer adoption benefits—many companies do. The military provides up to two thousand dollars per child when active-duty personnel adopt. There are also tax credits available to cover adoptions; adoption subsidies and grants are also available.

5. Choose an adoption agency.

You'll need to work with an agency in the state where you live. Contact several agencies to get a feel for which one would best suit your needs. Ask about their fees—including the fee for a home study (an in-house evaluation and orientation for prospective parents).

How do you find an agency?

- Contact the adoption specialist in your state for a list of local adoption agencies in your area.
- For private agencies, check the yellow pages under "Adoptions."
- Ask local adoption-support groups for their recommendations.

6. Notify your agency that you want to investigate further.

Depending on the agency, you may have to answer screening questions over the phone, or you may receive some literature that maps out the adoption process. Most likely you'll be invited to an orientation session for parents thinking about adoption.

7. Fill out an adoption application.

It's a good idea to attend the orientation session first before you fill out an application, which often comes with a nonrefundable application fee. The orientation should give you a good overview of the agency and the process, to make sure you're comfortable with the agency you've chosen.

8. Go through a home study.

This required step gives your social worker a chance to get to know you as well as prepare you for the adoption. You'll learn more about what to expect. Your agency will brief you on what you'll need for the home study, including documents such as marriage certificates, birth certificates, and personal references.

9. Attend adoption classes.

Most agencies provide adoption classes. These classes are a very helpful way to learn more about adoption issues as well as meet other adoptive parents.

10. Search for your child.

Your agency will search for a child for you. Some agencies publish photo-listing books of children waiting for homes:

11. Learn about your child.

After you've identified a child you'd like to adopt, you'll want to learn as much as possible about him or her. Talk with the social agency. Ask the agency if you can talk with the foster parents so you can arrange a smooth transition for your child.

The agency will help you arrange visits to your home to see how things fit for you and your child.

12. Get ready for your child: paperwork and preparation.

Check your family insurance plan. You'll want to make sure your policy is updated. Check into getting a new social security number and the original birth certificate for your child. It can be much more difficult to obtain a birth certificate after the adoption.

Prepare your other children for the changes. Talk it over with them, and prepare them for the transition.

13. Welcome your child home!

When your new child comes to your home, you become the temporary legal custodian. The agency will monitor how things are going for everyone. This evaluation time may take anywhere from a few weeks to a year.

14. File a petition to adopt.

Once everything checks out, you'll go to court to initiate an adoption petition for your child. You may need an attorney to help you.

15. Finalize the adoption.

This is the last step—finalization hearings. These hearings are a judicial proceeding and usually come within 6 to 12 months after your child is placed in your home. Typically, a hearing is only 10 to 30 minutes. This is when you are given permanent legal custody of your adopted child.

Remember back to high school when you were ready to change the world for the better? You've just made a great start. *You're changing the world of a child for the better.*

Notes

Notes

Notes

Notes

Notes

Notes

FOCUS ON THE FAMILY®

Welcome to the family!

Whether you purchased this book, borrowed it, or received it as a gift, we're glad you're reading it. It's just one of the many helpful, encouraging, and biblically based resources produced by Focus on the Family for people in all stages of life.

Focus began in 1977 with the vision of one man, Dr. James Dobson, a licensed psychologist and author of numerous best-selling books on marriage, parenting, and family. Alarmed by the societal, political, and economic pressures that were threatening the existence of the American family, Dr. Dobson founded Focus on the Family with one employee and a once-a-week radio broadcast aired on 36 stations.

Now an international organization reaching millions of people daily, Focus on the Family is dedicated to preserving values and strengthening and encouraging families through the life-changing message of Jesus Christ.

Focus on the Family Magazines

These faith-building, character-developing publications address the interests, issues, concerns, and challenges faced by every member of your family from preschool through the senior years.

| Focus on the Family **Citizen®** U.S. news issues | Focus on the Family **Clubhouse Jr.™** Ages 4 to 8 | Focus on the Family **Clubhouse™** Ages 8 to 12 | **Breakaway®** Teen guys | **Brio®** Teen girls 12 to 16 | **Brio & Beyond®** Teen girls 16 to 19 | **Plugged In®** Reviews movies, music, TV |

FOR MORE INFORMATION

 Online:
Log on to www.family.org
In Canada, log on to www.focusonthefamily.ca

Phone:
Call toll free: (800) A-FAMILY (232-6459)
In Canada, call toll free: (800) 661-9800

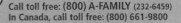